QUEER ACTION/QUEER IDEAS, A UNIQUE SERIES ADDRESSING
PIVOTAL ISSUES WITHIN THE LGBTQ MOVEMENT

BOOKS IN THE QUEER ACTION SERIES

Family Pride: What LGBT Families Should Know about Navigating Home, School, and Safety in Their Neighborhoods, by Michael Shelton

Out Law: What LGBT Youth Should Know About Their Legal Rights, by Lisa Keen

Come Out and Win: Organizing Yourself, Your Community, and Your World, by Sue Hyde

BOOKS IN THE QUEER IDEAS SERIES

Queer Virtue: What LGBTQ People Know About Life and Love and How It Can Revitalize Christianity, by the Reverend Elizabeth M. Edman

Love's Promises: How Formal and Informal Contracts Shape All Kinds of Families, by Martha M. Ertman

Gaga Feminism: Sex, Gender, and the End of Normal, by J. Jack Halberstam

God vs. Gay? The Religious Case for Equality, by Jay Michaelson

Queer (In)Justice: The Criminalization of LGBT People in the United States, by Joey L. Mogul, Andrea J. Ritchie, and Kay Whitlock

Beyond (Straight and Gay) Marriage: Valuing All Families Under the Law, by Nancy D. Polikoff

From the Closet to the Courtroom: Five LGBT Rights Lawsuits That Have Changed Our Nation, by Carlos A. Ball

At the Broken Places

*A Mother and Trans Son
Pick Up the Pieces*

**Mary Collins and
Donald Collins**

QUEER ACTION/QUEER IDEAS
A Series Edited by Michael Bronski

Beacon Press, Boston

BEACON PRESS
Boston, Massachusetts
www.beacon.org

Beacon Press books
are published under the auspices of
the Unitarian Universalist Association of Congregations.

20   19   18   17   8   7   6   5   4   3   2   1

This book is printed on acid-free paper that meets the uncoated paper
ANSI/NISO specifications for permanence as revised in 1992.

Text design and composition by Wilsted & Taylor Publishing Services

Some names and other identifying characteristics of people mentioned
in this work have been changed to protect their identities.

Library of Congress Cataloging-in-Publication Data

Names: Collins, Mary, author. | Collins, Donald, author.
Title: At the broken places : a mother and trans son pick up the pieces /
    Mary Collins and Donald Collins.
Description: Boston, Massachusetts : Beacon Press, [2017] | Series: Queer
    action/queer ideas | Includes bibliographical references.
Identifiers: LCCN 2016041965 (print) | LCCN 2016056899 (ebook) | ISBN
    9780807088357 (pbk. : alk. paper) | ISBN 9780807088364 (e-book)
Subjects: LCSH: Collins, Donald | Collins, Mary | Transgender
    youth—United States—Biography. | Transgender youth—Family
    relationships—United States. | Parents of transsexuals—United States. |
    Transgender people—Identity.
Classification: LCC HQ77.8.C65 C65 2017 (print) | LCC HQ77.8.C65 (ebook) |
    DDC 306.76/80835—dc23
LC record available at https://lccn.loc.gov/2016041965

For Constance Sullivan Collins
Mother & Grandmother

Contents

Authors' Notes

MARY COLLINS: *At the Broken Places* first started for me as something else that I submitted to a summer writing workshop at Yale.

"Your real story is on page eighteen of your essay," my classmates told me.

I thought I was writing about all sorts of unique forms of loss and grief in twenty-first-century life, but they made it clear that none of it was nearly as compelling as the section, buried on page eighteen, about the grief I felt as the mother of a daughter who was now a transgender son.

"I don't want to write about that," I told them.

"But that's your *real* story," they said.

There's no way I am revisiting that trauma, I thought, though I had to concede that I *had* brought the story up. On some deep level I yearned to process it and, more importantly, write the sort of book I had needed as a parent but never found.

Still, two more years went by, and the best I could muster was a rewrite of the original essay into the chapter that is now "Mapping Modern Grief" in this book. I started work on a few more pieces but knew that to do the whole story justice, I simply could not write the book alone. I needed Donald's point of view.

Three years after the Yale workshop, I asked him if he would join me on this project.

He had the courage and grace to say yes, despite all that had happened between us during his transition over his high school and college years. Much of it had not gone well; indeed, it nearly broke us as a family. But we both sensed that we had always needed a book like *At the Broken Places*, which digs into the muddy middle where we disagreed on so much, and we always knew we wanted to return to a loving, more empathetic space for each other. The majority of families with transgender children exist in this more conflicted space. Now, finally, I have mustered the emotional strength to share with them our *real* story.

DONALD COLLINS: When my mom asked me to go in on this book project with her, my initial reaction was the same as hers: heck no!

At the time, I was in the midst of my senior year of college, trying to burn through an overbooked schedule of five classes and a resident assistant job. My graduating class had cultivated a predictable air of dread surrounding our manic, uncertain futures. No one had jobs; some people had jobs; we hated them for having jobs; we hated ourselves for our jealousy.

Why would I want to write something about the past when I needed to invest all my energy in the present to worry about the future? Why would I go back into an emotionally charged space—the loaded back-and-forths between my mother and me, her trans son—when in a few weeks I would be making a literal escape from my East Coast history and driving to California?

But I didn't say no. I have never been a diary keeper, but on some level, I knew that writing about these exhausting years would help us, and maybe others. I did drive to California, and after locking down an apartment and work, I was ready to engage the proposal from my self-imposed distance.

For the five years leading up to my move, I had worked through, worked past, and, admittedly, held onto a lot of anger and sadness regarding how dysfunctional my family life turned when I came out as trans. As the relationship between my mother and me improved, I trusted these feelings to disappear, to expire. As Takeshi Kaneshiro's character muses in one of my favorite films, *Chungking Express*, "Is there anything on earth that doesn't expire?"

But these feelings didn't expire for me; they didn't expire for my mom either. It's only through communication, both within and without, that we can solve problems and move forward. I'm proud of the honest book we wrote, I'm proud of our collaboration, I'm proud that I said yes, and I'm proud that she asked.

Introductions

✦ ✦ ✦

✦ WORD BANK ✦

Gender is a social and cultural categorization of the body. Scholar and biologist Julia Serano uses "gender" in her book *Whipping Girl* to refer to "various aspects of a person's physical or social sex, their sex-related behaviors, the sex-based class system they are in," or any combination of these.

This gender categorization varies depending on time period and geographical location. The **gender binary** is a popular gender model that places bodies into two oppositional categories: men and women.

Queer is an umbrella term finding renewed popularity in the LGBTQ community. It originally meant "different" or "odd" and came to be used as a derogatory slur intended to shame homosexuality. Now "queer" is being reclaimed as a word that steps up to the plate when other labels fall short of describing an identity. In her 1996 book *Queer Theory: An Introduction*, scholar Annamarie Jagose explains "queer focuses on mismatches between gender, sex and desire."

Donald Collins

My mom keeps an extensive library at home, filling shelves with short-story collections or Shakespeare tomes. She'll talk about budgeting for a trip and then some package will arrive in the mail, an order of books she totally forgot about. I was always allowed to peruse her shelves as a kid, reading anything that interested me. When I was eleven she bought me a collection of David Sedaris's essays, in which, for the first time, I saw glimpses of myself.

Being trans and being gay are completely different things, and confusing the two has caused all of us no end of trouble. But like all identities, they do have intersections. Both face scrutiny for unwanted gender behavior; both are historically outsiders. Parents worry about boys that act *too* feminine, about girls who are *too* butch. So I marveled at the exploits of David Sedaris, this anxious young queer kid, even though I didn't quite know why the recognition was so strong.

Nowadays, my spacious apartment in California's San Fernando Valley has its own little queer library. It grew quite by accident: I enrolled in a gender studies course my sophomore year of college and got smacked with a substantial required reading list. Many of the books were out of print, so I found my way into the magical world of online used-book sellers. Most books for my media-centric courses demanded to be bought new, in such-and-such edition. They were dense, expensive, and, if I'm being honest, only cracked open before a test. After finals, my friends and I would line up to sell back our untouched titles to the bookstore in exchange for pocket money. But with this class, I didn't sell the books back, and I didn't donate them either. I liked them too much.

My used queer books arrived in dinged-up plastic bundles, dusty, sometimes with the old library cards still in the back. Most of them, whether novels or scholarly works, I had never even heard of: *Out of the Past*, by Neil Miller; *Dancer from the Dance*, by Andrew Holleran; *ZAMI: A New Spelling of My Name*, by Audre Lorde.

My mom cultivated this love of reading, a lifelong interest that buoyed me even when she and I were distant from each other, totally unreachable.

It seems only natural that I would compose a glossary for her, and for our readers, based not only on my own experiences but also my library. One of my very first trans books was the brightly colored *Transgender History*, by scholar Susan Stryker. Within her own extensive glossary, Stryker provides a way of looking at the word "transgender" that has stayed with me since my first reading three years ago.

Generally speaking, "trans" connotes someone who identifies with a gender other than the one assigned at birth. I was assigned "female" at birth, and now I identify as "male." This definition is pretty straightforward and often works in opposites. Boys become girls. Girls become boys. But Stryker calls the word back to its Latin roots, away from its attachment to the physical. She writes, "It is the movement across a socially imposed boundary away from an unchosen starting [place]."

None of us chooses our starting place. It's a sort of sister sentiment to those first lines in *The Great Gatsby*, "all the people in this world haven't had the advantages that you've had." Privilege is lottery and tradition. I have the privilege of being able bodied, upper middle class, white, well educated. Having the privilege of being assigned a gender we identify with is not something most people think about, because it's something most people have. I have so many privileges, but I don't have that one.

I love Stryker's definition of "trans" because it recaptures the word's true place as an umbrella term, beyond "boys" and "girls." There is incredible trepidation that comes with moving away from your starting place toward something else. It is exciting; it is horrifying. It is this form of "trans" that not only moved me but also moved the others in my life, away, away, away, to a place where we had no reliable guides and no right words.

For my mom and me, this book represents our best efforts, our worst shortcomings, and our frequent misunderstandings.

I hope someone, somewhere, can find it in a library—or put it in theirs—and feel that much less alone.

Mary Collins

We loved each other but needed a translator to help us communicate, and that translator never arrived.

I did not recognize the word "transgender" as it sprang from my daughter's lips; she came out to me in our kitchen during her final year of high school. I consider myself an urbane person, a strong advocate for equality for my many gay friends, but somehow I had never come in contact with the T on the LGBTQ continuum.

It hung there with full quotes around it, a three-dimensional thing that I am still staring at and trying to define.

In that moment, my daughter was trying to tell me that she wanted to abandon her given name and the feminine pronouns and replace them with a new thing, something more masculine and a better match for the person she saw in her own mind. Eventually, J. even gave away her body, but I did not consider such things then in that moment of confusion.

I know now, thanks to our memoir project, that Donald is not certain we should even be using the term "coming out," since a woman who does not feel like a woman, but rather like a man in a feminine body, is the one in the closet.

We are making up our own lexicon as we go along.

As a child, J. had a real knack for making up words that begged to be included in Webster's dictionary. While trying on new sneakers, she would complain that her socks felt "budgy" or, while eating, that some foods were "mooshie."

I found my daughter's knack for such invention great fun, the sign of a clever, creative mind. She ran language through her nimble vocal cords like music. When we moved from Connecticut to Baltimore, she was just eighteen months old and one day chatted away with a boy of the same age from across the street who had not yet said a word. They loved being together; she, rattling off tales and songs; he, the quiet, entertained listener. He stayed silent for three years, perhaps because my daughter had more than enough language for the both of them.

Such sweet tales about my ginger-haired, green-eyed girl now sit in mental storage, rarely retrieved out of deference to Donald, who finds any call back to his feminine self very stressful. I packed away photographs, old backpacks embroidered with his old name, any trace of *her*. I admit I balked at doing this. I was full of resentment, even though now I realize, as J. left to become Donald, she/he needed a clean slate. The downside of my intransigence was that, behind my back, he asked his high school teachers to start calling him by his new name and to refer to him with male pronouns, something I had begged him not to do. Wait until your first year of college, I said, when the shift will feel more natural and less dramatic.

The high school embraced him immediately. Counselors stepped up, teachers didn't hesitate; none of them spoke to me.

Dialogue between Donald and me deteriorated with each new word ripped from my daily vocabulary—*daughter, she, her, girl, woman*. I feared these small edits would lead to a cascade of changes.

And I was right.

Donald could not spend the rest of his life walking around asking everyone to use his male name and male pronouns when referring to him. He wanted simply to *be* a man and that required fundamental physical changes.

Binding. Hormones. Top surgery. The lexicon continued to expand, and I simply did not grasp any of it. Actions I labeled as rash, impatient, and even mentally unhinged, he defined as essential to his evolving—and fragile—sense of identity. If he did not want J., and there was no J., then who was Donald? If he did not craft something to take J.'s place, he was nothing. As good as dead.

Sadly, by some estimates, more than 40 percent of transgender children attempt suicide. I knew the stakes but lacked the fluency to remedy the situation. I'd use the wrong pronoun and see Donald rage. I bluntly disagreed with his decision to take steroids. He felt thwarted by me in his effort to transition from female to male. I refused to pay for any surgeries because I considered him too young to make such radical, irreversible decisions. He contemplated severing his ties with me for good.

Even the word "transition" became fraught. That's not what Donald calls it, since he is not leaving something solid for something else. He is leaving something he feels he never should have been in the first place. In one of his essays in this book, he writes of his past self as though she were a sister. Can a former self be a sibling? Maybe in some "Lost Her, Found Him" dictionary that's the one best compromise, a way to avoid the complete erasure of something I'd held as a baby and loved with a joy I will never forget.

Family members, old friends from J.'s childhood, new friends from Donald's present, doctors, counselors, and educators all added their own terms to the Transgender Tower of Babel. The professionals in particular lacked a language that included me, the questioning parent opposed to the physical changes my child wanted to undergo. When I spoke about the grief I felt over my "lost" daughter, a counselor told me to keep such feelings to myself because my transgender son would feel judged.

The new friends, who never knew J. so did not miss her, took Donald in with a verve that startled, something I know that filled him with gratitude but which I considered a fundamental affront to my rights as a parent. These friends never spoke to me. The silence worked like aggressive body language in my life, a form of shunning that I found nearly as devastating as the growing divide between Donald and myself as he lowered his voice, removed his breasts, continued to take steroids.

Judge, jury, verdict. How fitting that people, especially medical professionals, used such legal sounding terms, because when they erased my right to question, they erased my right to parent. I know that many transgender individuals face horrible harassment and marginalization, but my experience with Donald was precisely the opposite. An entire group of people stepped into his new verbal landscape and hugged his new identity with great openness and sincerity. I am now able to feel some semblance of awe at their broadness of spirit, but they went so far down that end of the continuum that they left no space for me.

Feeling like a stranger in your own family dynamic is a dangerous place to be, not only for a parent but also for transgender children, because they find themselves cut off from the only solid land they've stood on before building their new foundation. The whirl of people around us simply failed to see that crafting some sort of neutral space for my transgender son and me to speak to each other was the best thing they could have done with their energies. The goal should be to have the entire unit come to better terms before it's too late, as it almost was for Donald and me.

When I asked Donald to collaborate on a memoir with me on four core subject areas that kept rising up in my life as the parent of a transgender child—pronouns and body parts; my sense of loss versus his sense of discovery; the disclosure game I felt we were always playing; and our shifting sense of rights as parent and child—I was really asking him to tap into that creative space he once lived in as a child when he made up words with such smart flair.

This book represents the neutral territory we created, where we call back and forth to each other about things that nearly destroyed us. I gained more empathy for what Donald went through and why, and he gained more empathy for me.

Pronouns and Body Parts

✦ ✦ ✦

✦ WORD BANK ✦

Gender dysphoria refers to deep dissatisfaction with one's gender or aspects thereof, often body-centric. This is a wildly popular term for both trans people and health-care professionals to use to describe a feeling of misalignment. It is the official "trans" diagnosis in the current edition of the *Diagnostic and Statistical Manual of Mental Disorders* (*DSM*).

However, Julia Serano challenges the term effectively, arguing that "gender dysphoria" is an "extrinsic matter" regarding the severe stress trans folk experience from *outside* gender expectations. She suggests a better term would be *gender dissonance*, which reflects the "cognitive dissonance experienced by trans people due to a misalignment of their subconscious and physical sexes." This dissonance can generate significant emotional pain, depression, and hopelessness.

Transition seeks to describe the social, physical, emotional, and medical aspects of moving from one gender to another. Some trans people pursue *gender-confirming surgery* (*GCS*) as part of their transition. GCS replaces the outdated "sex-reassignment surgery" and applies to any surgical procedure intended to better align the recipient's body and gender identity. Many trans people still resent the medical agenda that promotes surgery as necessary to "confirm" their gender.

Who Wears the Pants?

Donald Collins

> Clothes are but a symbol of something hid deep beneath.
> —Virginia Woolf, *Orlando*

For eight months, I worked part time at a popular museum in downtown Los Angeles. The customer-service work was simultaneously mind-numbing and exhausting, but the staff was amazing, and you couldn't beat the atmosphere. Our clientele consisted largely of families, school groups, and college students on second dates.

One morning, my coworker Yolanda tapped my arm to point out a particularly dysfunctional family, the two youngest members fleeing in all directions as their parents burned with embarrassment. The mom took a firm line while the dad observed. She got everyone regrouped.

"You know who wears the pants in that relationship," Yolanda remarked with a grin.

"But they're all wearing pants," I said. "Even the children are wearing pants."

We laughed the hollow laugh of minimum-wage employees and got back to work.

Yolanda knew my jibe had intended to diffuse the stereotypical phrase, and I, knowing my friend, understood that she meant the comment as praise. She was admiring the woman's focus and grit in the face of unruly kids and an unhelpful spouse. But putting "the pants" on the wife insinuates her behavior as unnatural or unfeminine. *Look at that woman acting like a man!* The joke relies on the gender stereotypes surrounding the roles of men and women in a heterosexual relationship.

It may seem like a ridiculous piece of overthinking, picking apart the situation this way, but when piled on top of each other, vignettes like this add up to something bigger, and even more ridiculous.

At seventeen, if one of those wayward kids at the museum had kept asking me "Why? Why? Why?" on the subject of gender or gender roles, I'd struggle to turn up anything except an exasperated "Because!"

✦ ✦ ✦

"So do you have a penis now?"

The question came lazily out of my friend Jerry's mouth, as if he was asking for a piece of gum. I was seventeen, newly out at my boarding school, and completely unprepared for the prying minds (and eyes) of my peers.

We were hanging out on the set of a classmate's final photography project, a series of portraits. The sheer screen, hot lights, and tripods made me feel even more on the spot.

"I—I haven't had surgery yet," I stammered back.

"Oh," he said, with something like disappointment. "Are you going to?"

✦ ✦ ✦

By coming out in my dorm, and subsequently my classes, I had made my gender public information. My protective dorm head, Mrs. A., had warned me as much.

"Tomorrow morning the kids will all be texting about it," she said, the sentence a peak specimen of 2011.

For most of the community at the Loomis Chaffee School, in Windsor, Connecticut, I doubt my coming out caused an immediate shift in the way they saw gender; rather, I was an exception. They cared about me as an individual, and honored my wishes by respecting my name and pronoun change. And although they did respect me, it was entirely within their power to willfully disregard my request. I was nervous every time the subject of my gender came up because I deeply felt this vulnerability. While I had given my classmates the straightforward information they needed to respect me, I had also given them the information they needed to hurt me.

A high school friend of mine who later came out as trans recently posted a Facebook status about his difficulties with this dynamic. He was having trouble at his job. "I'm tired of having no control over who knows I'm trans, over who knows my birth name, and how they use that information," he vented. "Apparently trans people don't get the luxury of privacy."

Today, people I hardly know ask me about my birth name, my sex life, or my surgical history. Trans people commiserate about these things, because no matter how different we all are, the questions we get are often the same. And while now I accept that being a visible trans person means having to deal with spam, back in high school I had no idea why people suddenly felt they had an all-access pass to scrutinize my anatomy.

Let's get back to my penis.

✦ ✦ ✦

Unlike "What was your girl name?" asking someone "Do you have a penis?" is a bit . . . bolder. It has the dizzying effect of being alternately very intimate and very depersonalizing. Intimate because it asks about your literal intimates, and depersonalizing because it speaks to only that part of you, not to you as a whole.

Unless you are romantically or sexually involved with me, or treating me for a life-threatening penis-related emergency, you shouldn't ask me if I have a penis.

✦ ✦ ✦

Jerry was the first person to ask me the penis question, an honor that I haven't ever let him know about. While now one of the most vocal LGBTQ advocates I know, at the time he was a sophomore at Loomis, a fifteen-year-old operating with understandably limited information about what "trans" meant. I still genuinely believe his inquiry was part curiosity and part small talk. *What do trans people care about? What does my trans friend care about?*

During high school, I navigated the overwhelming emotions surrounding my gender with a limited amount of skill and information. I felt like a first-year college student who accidentally wanders into the wrong classroom and gets mistaken for the professor. As I mention in another essay, this feeling of being the sole ambassador for an identity or a subject—and being completely unprepared for it—is terrifying and isolating. I could speak to my personal experiences, but I couldn't contextualize them, I couldn't diffuse inappropriate questions or even understand why they were inappropriate.

"[Being] trans does not come with a diploma," my cousin Oscar once wrote, "although that would be nice."

When Jerry asked me if I had a penis, whether he realized it or not, he was experimenting with a way of looking at me. Through various reactions of my friends, my family, my professors, I began to piece together an outside picture of what I looked like. I wasn't just discovering what it meant to me to be trans; I was finding out what being trans meant to the people in my community.

✦ ✦ ✦

"Have you had . . . ?" the nurse nodded down at her own nether region, apparently too much of a professional to say the phrase "dick surgery." I recalled that Monty Python sketch. *Nudge nudge, wink wink.*

It was Halloween my sophomore year of college, and I lay stiffly in a small bed, wearing a hospital gown. The room wasn't really a room but one of those curtained-off ER cubbies. I had a distinct fear of losing consciousness and being unable to fend off nurse "Margie's" curiosity. I regretted, and still do, not asking a friend to come with me.

"You know," Margie continued, "I never would have known."

She effortlessly broached my gender but stopped short of naming it, of using any of the words. I was in pain, around a 6 on that emoji pain chart (the face that looks constipated), and my politeness shield was slipping. I wanted to play dumb and force her to spit it out. You never would have known *what?* What the *fuck* do you want from me?

But instead I said, "Oh, thank you."

My haunted maze began hours earlier, when an abdominal pain caught my attention during French class. I thought I might be hungry, because I'm always hungry, so I waited out the period. But by the time class ended, the pain was so severe I couldn't stand straight. A friend accompanied my mysterious ailment and me to the health center, where, finding no answers, the staff quickly had campus police drive me to the around-the-block emergency room. Expecting appendicitis, I found the actual diagnosis even more startling: a ruptured ovarian cyst.

At the time of my ER visit, I had yet to have top surgery, and without my binders (two compression vests I wore), I felt totally exposed. Over my billowy gown, I bunched up the bed sheets for camouflage. The orderly who wheeled me in for an ultrasound sensed my trepidation.

"You know, I had one of those cysts a few weeks ago, in my stomach," he said kindly, "Had my ultrasound here too. It's not that unusual."

I wondered if the nurses had asked him about his penis.

We think of bodies as being distinctly sexed under "male" or "female," but in the medical sense, I was neither. I found myself occupying a strange no-man's land in the hospital's system. In this situation, it was essential for me to come out as trans in order to receive proper, efficient treatment. And unlike many trans people, I did receive proper, efficient treatment. Despite Margie's initially probing questions, no one asked me to strip unnecessarily; no one conducted non-essential examinations or touched me inappropriately.

In the National Gay and Lesbian Task Force's 2010 survey of 6,450 trans and gender-nonconforming people, 19 percent reported being denied medical treatment because of their gender identification; 28 percent reported "harassment" in medical settings. One of my mentors once recalled being loudly summoned by his birth name in front of the waiting room of a new doctor's office. Some of my closest friends have experienced traumatic medical consultations and appointments they will never speak about.

I was released from the ER that night, and after the pain subsided,

I trick-or-treated with my friends in Beacon Hill and then went out for burgers. The physical ordeal was officially over, but it set in motion a troublesome, non-penis-related train of thought: Did I want my ovaries? Did I want my uterus? Did I want biological children? Did I have other questions beyond that I had neglected to confront? And, perhaps most immediately, did I want to risk another adventure like this?

My decision to pursue a hysterectomy my senior year of college was personal, based on my individual relationship with my body, my organs, and our future together. I had been out as trans for almost four years, maintained hormone treatment, and in 2013, the year prior, I processed a legal name change and underwent top surgery. I had come a long way to understanding what being male meant to me. For the first time, I truly grasped that there is no right way to be trans, that there is no right way to "feel" any gender. So at this point in my life, I didn't believe that having a uterus impeached my masculinity. I didn't want the surgery because these were "female" organs and I, a guy, wanted them gone. Rather than feeling dysphoric with my reproductive system, I began to feel that my reproductive system was dysphoric with me. I began to feel that those parts of my body were unhappy and, in a way, unwelcomed.

The ER doctor suggested that testosterone might have contributed to the development of the ovarian cyst. It terrified me that the same hormone treatment that improved my quality of life so much might now be threatening my well-being. I cannot know for sure that this was the cause, only that polycystic ovaries are an occasional risk with trans men who take hormones.

I was, and still am, conflicted over the fact that I had to choose between my future health and my ability to have biological kids. It's the choice I resent more than the having-kids thing. I know I can have an incredible family of my own, and that it will be no more or less real. Many trans people who undergo hysterectomies will extract a sample of their genetic material beforehand or save one ovary for later.

It is in the midst of difficult decisions like this that I am struck by everyone's continued preoccupation with dicks and vaginas. The national conversation has diversified, but even in the transmasculine community, having a "penis" is a massive topic, a measure of manliness. Trans and non-trans people alike will often assume that surgery, specifically the downstairs variety, is a desired endgame, if not *the* endgame.

A college administrator once recommended me to a trans group in the Boston area, and prior to my top surgery I set up a meeting with its coordinator to get advice about insurance. Completely unsolicited, he recommended me to a phalloplasty surgeon, even offering to pull down his pants and show me the results up close and personal.

"Not even the doctors can tell," he bragged as I mentally plotted my escape.

✦ ✦ ✦

I spent winter break of senior year recovering from a total hysterectomy in my cousin Oscar's basement.

The "hysto" involved only four tiny cuts instead of the long abdominal incision many patients still endure. The technical name for this surgery is "laproscopically assisted vaginal hysterectomy (LAVH)," which really means "two surgeons and their little camera take all your reproductive organs away."

The recovery, as my primary surgeon, Dr. T., described, is like having "the period from hell." I would argue it actually is more like the aftermath of an "ab workout from hell," but aside from the core soreness and bloating, I felt tremendous joy and relief. Completing the hysto meant clearing a major medical hurdle, counteracting the threat of further cysts as well as ovarian and cervical cancer.

"All your intestines will move about two inches down after the procedure," Dr. T. explained, "to take advantage of the new space."

His words evoked a reality-TV couple celebrating their housing renovation: *We demolished the downstairs bathroom, and you wouldn't believe how far the kitchen expanded!*

After my top surgery the summer prior, I was constantly bumping into things as I got used to my new sense of equilibrium. But that winter, my body was doing most of the adjusting on the inside. The next two weeks were made of molasses. I moved slowly, sat and reclined even slower, and couldn't lift anything. I prematurely fretted about people hugging me too strongly when the break ended.

Oscar made this amazing iced tea with like a hundred ginger tea bags and dark honey, and I drank it constantly, pouring it greedily out of a little green teapot. During Oscar's school days, I slept late, went for short walks, and read. At night, we watched *The X-Files* and ate popcorn. It was a sleepy, hobbit-like existence. Incredibly, the recovery felt like a holiday.

The long hours of quietude allowed me to eulogize all the busy ones that preceded them. Waves of nostalgia permeated my Oxycodone daze, hung over my morning toast, clouded up my two o'clock showers. I thought about being a person in perpetual translation of himself, and about the world that was constantly translating me. I thought about penises and vaginas and happy trails and pierced ears and letters on driver's licenses and passports. I thought about haircuts and painted fingernails and cologne samples and late nights at the gym.

✦ ✦ ✦

Since coming out at Loomis almost exactly four years prior to my hysto, I had relentlessly schemed and organized to make my life as Donald possible. Now all of it was over. My "transition" wasn't over, but this specific part of my journey was. The closest thing I can compare it to emotionally would be my high school graduation.

I had so much to return to at Emerson College, in Boston: my first choice of classes, a wonderful network of friends, a fraternity, being part of an RA staff and having my own room. But a piece of me was scared now that I filed and sealed the paperwork and removed all the gauze. I worried that being trans was the only thing that I was. I worried that without all the prescriptions and consultations, I was empty and directionless. I found myself somehow believing that "trans" was everything good and bad about me at the same time.

I occasionally fixate angrily on the idea that my personal identity "accomplishments" are solutions to problems I should never have had. I shouldn't have *had* to remove my ovaries because I shouldn't have been *born* with them in the first place. I shouldn't have *had* to orchestrate a medically induced puberty; I should have been born *male*. This line of thinking brings out the worst in me, and I find myself regressing to crude ideas of men and women, penises and vaginas. I feel nothing but bitter and hateful towards the queer parts of myself, when really I am grateful for all the ways being trans has expanded my life. Bitterness and hate are motivators, but they won't make a body strong, and they won't care for it day in and day out.

At Emerson I had the opportunity to pursue a minor in women's and gender studies. I took classes where, for the first time, I learned about feminist theory, gender theory, and sexuality in depth. My academic work expanded my awareness and responsibility, but it was during that sleepy week of post-op at Oscar's house that I really put everything together.

I wasn't synthesizing scholarly arguments about what gender is and isn't. I was fully confronting the experience of being thrust into an emotional and physical space where gender was the primary totem of my existence. For years, it was all I thought about, and all I thought other people thought about when they looked at me or talked to me (or about me). I was exhausted because it was exhausting.

✦ ✦ ✦

So where was my mother in all this? And why have I used the word "penis" thirteen times?

✦ ✦ ✦

In coming out to my mom, and sharing my plans for medical treatment with her, I was navigating two major areas of conflict. The first was my mother's difficulty with the concept of "trans" as it applied to me, and the second was her deep parental attachment to my physical self.

As a single parent, my mother's position was compounded by the intensity of her bond with an only "daughter." It had been us against the world for so long. Not only did my coming out essentially call into question everything my mother knew about me as a person; it also felt like a rejection of what she had given me: my body, my name, my role as daughter.

"It's like you're asking me to be in the room when you shoot yourself," she said, weeping, during one of our earliest conversations.

In changing my name, cutting my hair, throwing out old clothes, starting hormone replacement treatment, undergoing top surgery and then a hysterectomy, I imagined that, to my mother, J. died by degrees. It's taken me a while to realize there wasn't a single moment when my mother "lost" her daughter but a period of four to five years when every time she saw me, something was gone or had changed. I wasn't, broadly speaking, a different person, but my signs were different.

Aside from my grandmother, most of my family is what I'd called Holiday Irish Catholics. *Some* of us go to church *sometimes*, but "religious" is not one of our top identifiers. Yet when I came out, many of my mother's fears seemed to come from a deeply Christian place. She told me, on more than one occasion, that to undergo hormone treatment and surgery would be unnatural, against God in some way. Despite all our progress together, despite her agreement that my decisions have improved my quality of life, we still clash on the "physical changes" front.

Much like that of my schoolmates, the Collinses' overall reaction to my transness happened on the individual-as-exception level. They tried to change the way they referred to me because it mattered to me, not necessarily because they *believed* my masculine identity. I don't want to suggest that the individual approach isn't important; it's essential. You don't have to have far-reaching or radical ideas about gender to call someone the right name. But because I was dealing with larger issues, including creating my identity and surviving the process, I began to become impatient with my family's response. My mother, aunts, uncles, and cousins *were* trying to understand, struggling. I just couldn't manage their discomfort and my own at the same time.

✦   ✦   ✦

By the time I had top surgery, in my junior year of college, I had been on testosterone for around three years. "T" is a naturally occurring hormone that appears in varying levels in *all* biological sexes. A monitored schedule of T injections aimed to trick my body into halting the production of estrogen as its primary hormone, and adjust my secondary sex characteristics accordingly. T launched me into a second puberty. My voice dropped; I began to redistribute weight and muscle and grow facial hair. My appetites changed; I sometimes slept for ten, twelve hours at a time. I'll admit I found myself unable to cry for almost a year and unable to remember dreams at all. My daily moods reached a more constant, upbeat elevation.

The morph in physiology through hormones is the most known arc in the trans-guy narrative, even more than the penis stuff. It's the moment when people think of trans boys as becoming Real Boys, or at least looking like them. And for a long time, I believed testosterone made me real too. What it actually did was give me a real *relationship* with my body for the first time, a connection that spurred me on to a love of fitness and cooking, and improved my sense of personal style. Not everyone needs hormone treatment for this to happen.

✦   ✦   ✦

While the "concept" piece of my trans identity was at the center of our disagreement during high school, the "physical changes" argument between my mother and me ramped up freshman year of college. I began my testosterone regimen, which segued into a six-month semi-estrangement. We exchanged a few terse e-mails but didn't speak to or see each other, despite being only a two-hour drive apart. My mom didn't feel emotionally capable of seeing me or having me stay with her if I was taking hormones. The full extent of all our distances from each other reverberated back and forth unpredictably.

We reunited the summer before my sophomore year in my hometown of Alexandria, Virginia. I was working with friends at a summer camp and living with my stepfather. The reconciliation was tentative and quiet. The disagreements continued, but this time so did the communication.

✦ ✦ ✦

It's horrifying when something that gives you great fulfillment has the exact opposite effect on someone you care about. For every answer you demand to find in yourself, there is a complementary question directed outward: *If they really loved me, why wouldn't they be happy for me? Don't they trust me to make the right decisions? Is their love conditional? Am I really hurting them or are they choosing to react this way?*

✦ ✦ ✦

Reconnection and believing in reconnection seem simple, but they aren't things you can schedule or predict. It's hard, and there are no guarantees.

✦ ✦ ✦

My grandmother used to say (and still does; she's ninety-two) that if we could just "keep the lines of communication open," my mom and I would one day understand each other a little better. Like two busy people just blindly ringing each other up, timing always wrong, after hours or on hold, until one day we *connect.* And this connection doesn't mean forgiveness or acceptance or even agreement of any kind.

It just means two people who are finally ready to be on the phone.

✦ WORD BANK ✦

At birth, **sex** is assigned to a baby based on anatomical reproductive organs and genitalia. **Gender identity** refers to one's inner sense of gender. Gender role is associated with the behavior expected from different sexes in society.

Mismatch

Mary Collins

Sex Assigned at Birth

We all begin as female in the womb.

Eggs fertilized by a sperm with a Y chromosome eventually develop into boys, but nature's original template is the female body, breasts included.

What did I know about the gender of my first and only child when I delivered my baby? Based on the simple biology of external private parts, I had a girl. I named her J. and used female pronouns whenever I spoke about her.

Right from the start, J. proved extremely sensitive to the texture of fabrics, as well as quick to respond emotionally to loud noises, too much activity, and anything remotely menacing, like a spooky-looking stuffed animal. Scientists have shown that these traits are inherently more common in female babies.

✦ ✦ ✦

As J.'s mother, I am an athletic woman, ambidextrous, dyslexic; I hear pitch differently in my left ear versus my right and am quite gifted at parallel parking. These traits appear much more frequently in men (though there's still some controversy about the parallel parking).

But I never felt my gender did not match my body.

By age twelve, J. started deliberately constructing a gender-neutral look using the tools available to any middle school kid: haircut, type of shoes, size of watch.

By sixteen, J. had moved onto the name and switched to Donald, and asked teachers to start referring to her with male pronouns.

By eighteen, Donald began hormone treatment to lower his voice. After six to eight weeks the shift is irreversible, because the vocal cords thicken.

By twenty-one, Donald told me he needed to remove his ovaries and possibly his uterus for a range of reasons, including the increased risk of cancer caused by the male hormones he was taking. In an effort to balance out the mismatch between his mind and his body, he had to resort to a toxic hormonal brew. The conflicting signals created side effects.

I remained skeptical that such a mismatch could ever occur, but eventually learned from research and interviews with psychologists that boy fetuses develop their physical traits—a penis, for example—about eight weeks after conception, but their brains are flooded with male hormones again at about six months, which shapes their *perception* of their own gender. Nature actually takes two steps to build a man that looks *and* identifies as male. The possibility for disconnect is built into the process.

Does that mean a child of, say, twelve should have the right to alter his or her body with hormones and surgery to change his or her gender? How young is too young? Is it better for someone to wait until at least the mid-twenties, when the mind and capacity for understanding cause and effect are fully developed, or does it become ever more difficult the longer the person waits to transition and, perhaps, raises an already high risk for suicide?

Of course, many even question the right to make the transition at all.

Some long-term studies, mainly done by Swedish scientists, have tended to muddy rather than clarify the answers. Even after gender-reassignment surgery, transgender people are at much higher risk for suicide. And some studies have showed that many young children with a conflicted sense of gender identity often lose their desire to alter their sex and grow up to be gay.

Oophorectomy—ovarian-removal surgery. The word itself sounds Dr. Seuss-like, with the O, O, P, H, O, spelling that captures for me the quixotic medical advice Donald received. Something deep within him drove him forward. Doctors and counselors wanted to help him grab the holy grail of a balanced personal identity, but I also knew that Donald was thirty times more likely to die of a heart attack after he removed his ovaries than of ovarian cancer if he'd kept them.

My own ob-gyn told me this and said she would never perform the surgery. In previous conversations with this doctor over the years, she had said her practice did not perform any gender-transition-related surgeries, but during my latest visit, she revealed that one of the doctors in her practice now handles such things.

Such things.

But ovaries and a uterus are not things—which is such a gender-neutral word—they are part of one's gender. Donald quickly disabused me of my antiquated attitudes and opted not for an oophorectomy but a full-blown hysterectomy at age twenty-two, because his swollen uterus pressed against his other organs, causing great discomfort, and he rightly feared another burst ovarian cyst.

My own mother had a hysterectomy in her early fifties because a pap smear had shown the early stages of cancer; she almost hemorrhaged to death in the operating room. I remember the parents of my best friend at the time telling me they would care for me if my mother died (I was thirteen, and at the time, both my parents were in the hospital in intensive care, my mother, recovering after her surgery, and my father, dying of cancer).

In my universe, cancer is pretty much the only reason why anyone would slice out body parts and risk bleeding out on an operating table. In Donald's world, his biology was the cancer, and he rejoiced that he could use modern medicine to eliminate it.

The doctor made small incisions on either side of Donald's abdomen to remove the ovaries and suck out the uterus, a procedure known as laparoscopic surgery, considered minimally invasive (ah, the irony). Swift, clean (no six-inch scars), and, from Donald's point of view, an amazing success.

His body felt the new clarity almost immediately. No more bloating. Better moods. Better energy. No more swollen ovaries.

During the same span of time Donald elected to carve out his maleness, my own estrogen and progesterone levels gradually dropped as I entered menopause. I expected hot flashes (true), vaginal dryness (no), a lower sex drive (barely), mood swings (actually my moods stabilized).

What I experienced instead was a slight weight gain, larger breasts, an evening out of my temperament, a softening of my personality over all, a rise in my empathy for others, and a greater sensitivity to loud noises, rough fabrics, and strong smells. (I still parallel park well.)

Donald's surgically and chemically induced "second puberty," between the ages of eighteen and twenty-two, seemed to more directly match the scientists' prediction for my natural menopause. He became more like me in the alpha-woman androgynous stages of my twenties and thirties, and I became more like Donald when he was J., a sensitive, intellectual, artistic girl.

All the scientific studies in the world will never pin down what it means to be male or female. None of us inhabit our gender the same way decade after decade.

Just as my only child was about to graduate college and launch into full adulthood as a working, self-sufficient person, I came into my own as a heterosexual female in my fifties with some masculine tendencies that I embrace rather than hide. My daughter now feels infinitely more comfortable as a trans man stripped of the feminine biology nature bestowed on her/him at birth.

Gender Identity

Facebook has more than fifty categories for gender. I teach at a nearby state university and when I told one of my college classes this, none of the students believed me and had never heard of most of the terms listed on the site: *agender/neutrois, androgyne/androgynous, bigender, cisgender, female to male (FTM), gender fluid, intersex, male to female (MTF)* . . .

I scanned what the students were wearing and saw pink sweatshirts on the women and dark-blue tops on the men, lightweight pointy toed shoes on the women and sneakers on the men. None of them wore any of the super-expensive designs from Prada, Marni, and Giorgio Armani, all of which had just launched gender-neutral lines featured in the slick pages of the *New York Times Magazine* under a story titled "One." In my students' day-to-day lives, the gender stereotypes I've experienced all my life remain startling in place.

Those aged fifteen to twenty-five are leading the charge for a more gender-fluid vocabulary, but they represent a tiny subset of that age group. From what I see in my classes, the majority of young people remain remarkably disengaged from and even oblivious to the most significant linguistic shift in my lifetime.

In 2015 the *New York Times* officially introduced the title "Mx." for individuals who do not want to be clearly identified as male or female. The *Washington Post* now accepts "they" as a pronoun for gender-fluid people. Other mass media markets have followed suit. As a young woman growing up in the 1970s, I remember the debate over the title "Ms.," used so women no longer had to identify their marital status. While researching these changes I came across the interesting fact that "you" was the plural of "thou." Languages are meant to evolve.

But for reasons I have not yet fathomed, I embrace Ms. but struggle with the idea of eliminating male and female pronouns as identifying markers. Discerning if a person is a man or a woman remains important to me as I navigate social interactions. My relationship with Donald has forced me, for the first time, to ask myself "Why?" When I mention to my classes that I am writing a book with my transgender son about our lives, they generally look uncomfortable and remain silent. According to a study done by YouGov, Americans under age thirty are far less likely to consider being transgender as morally wrong than, say, citizens over age sixty-five (more than one in three believe that), but somehow

I still don't see that more open mindset among the young people I deal with, other than a very vocal minority.

College admissions offices have started to anticipate the cultural shift my own students don't see coming. Brown University and the University of Vermont, to name just two, no longer ask students to check if they are male or female; instead they ask them to select their gender identity. At the University of Vermont, one student received approval to be officially referred to as "they." Many dorms offer gender-neutral floors with gender-neutral bathrooms, clearly a step ahead of states like North Carolina. Donald's college health-insurance program covered the cost of his gender-reassignment surgery, and other states have started requiring all insurers to follow suit.

Some languages embrace a gender continuum. The Swedes added the gender-neutral pronoun *hen* to official dictionaries in 2015 to substitute for *boys* and *girls*; they especially encourage preschools to use *hen* to guard against stereotyping kids at an early age. In the Philippines, to cite another example, the Tagalog word for gender, *kasarian*, translates more accurately as "kind or species." Even though the root for gender in English also sprang from a word that meant "kind," today our language remains firmly in the world of *his/her/he/she/man/woman*. It or *they*, which one of Donald's trans friends prefers, just seems to sit there oddly on the page, and when spoken, seems to bust open and misshape the rules of grammar.

It is going to college now.

They like school.

But Donald's experience has made me rethink even my native tongue, which I work with for a living as a writer and teacher of writing. Of course many grammatical rules can be seen as arbitrary, but others prove necessary for communication and form the foundation of a common language. From nature's point-of-view, if "nature" can even have one, most species need a distinct male and distinct female to procreate.

But not all.

In many parts of Europe—Germany, for example—there's a strong movement toward a post-gender world with gender-neutral bathrooms, neutral pronouns in the classroom, even rigorous rules against gender stereotyping in billboard ads! For some odd reason the American media never seems to bring up trends in other countries and instead portrays gender-related changes—such as the call for legislation to allow transgender individuals to use the bathroom that matches their self-designated gender—as some boundary-pushing exercise. Progress is taking place all around the world, and it can seem sometimes as if the United States is lagging behind. But, to be honest, there are so many other, more important issues to worry about for transgender individuals and their families.

Today, when members of the military and their families tend to lean conservative on issues such as LGBTQ rights, I must remind myself that the US military has often taken the lead when it comes to opening doors to people of color, women, and immigrants. It would be easy to wax patriotic about the laudable track record, but usually recruitment came down to supply and demand. During World War II, for example, my mother was mocked in her small New England town for volunteering to serve in the Navy, but the huge manpower shortage meant the country actually needed her services. As a WAVE, a member of the Women's Reserves, she took on jobs, such as drafting maps, rarely open to women before.

While putting the final touches on this book in 2016, I learned that President Barack Obama appointed Eric Fanning as the first openly gay secretary of the army, a shift I never could have imagined occurring in my lifetime. The military has also softened its stance on allowing transgender soldiers to serve openly, rather than under the shadow of "Don't Ask, Don't Tell." But such progress doesn't change my overall feeling that "military" = "conservative" and "conservative" = "vehemently uncomfortable with transgender individuals."

Before Donald went off to New York City for a paid internship at age twenty-one, I pulled up a map of voting patterns in the United States and looked at red districts versus blue districts and told him that *there*—pointing to large cities—his gender-bending ways probably wouldn't matter all that much, but *there*—pointing to the rural South— they could be deadly.

He. She. It. They. Drunken, gun-toting men have beaten trans people and left them for dead over that shifting continuum.

Of course something resembling acceptance has broken out in the media, with trans woman Laverne Cox, from the hit TV show *Orange Is the New Black*, on the cover of *Time* magazine; another TV show, *Transparent*, winning an Emmy; and, of course, Caitlyn (formerly Bruce) Jenner's transition playing out across every possible media outlet, from Twitter to the morning talk shows. In recent years, there has been a rush of TV shows, documentaries, books, and movies about trans people, but it all feels very voyeur-like, with glib black-and-white discussions about whether transgender people are sinful or the next group to press for their civil rights.

What we need is a third way to talk about gender issues, dialogue that is not so polarizing but more in line with what really happens when people slip along the gender slide rule. Instead of asking if gender nonconformity is right or wrong, we could be discussing what it is, what it means, and how much pain it can cause for the person in transition and those who love that person.

How do we all stay in motion without hurting each other?

Most parents of young girls worry about protecting them from sexual predators, sexual harassment, and risks on social media, but I never worried about my vulnerable red-haired, fair-eyed young daughter as much as I worry about my trans son. I do not agree with the decisions he has made to alter his body so completely and at such a young age, but that does not negate my love for him or my concern for his right to remain protected.

He seeks an authentic self.

He seeks to match his gender with his identity.

A short haircut and name change were not enough for him.

But gender dystopia remains listed in the *Diagnostic and Statistical Manual of Mental Disorders* (*DSM*), the bible of psychiatric disorders (they ditched homosexuality as a mental illness in 1973 after much debate), and the search for scientific clarity on whether or not transgender people are mentally ill or genetically predetermined continues internationally. The Dutch have led the way in research, studying how brain structure impacts gender identity, for example, and there's the Gender Identity Research and Education Society and the World Professional Association for Transgender Health (WPATH), which emphatically challenges listing transgender people as mentally ill and says that being trans "should not be judged as inherently pathological or negative."

But it's hard to see any path to understanding and acceptance, never mind WPATH, when your own child comes out as transgender and you have never heard of that word. The lack of general education around all of this hurts families.

It's hard to see a path when the daughter you love dissolves before your eyes and every high school advisor, counselor, and medical professional who helps her do that cannot talk to you because of privacy issues for young adults sixteen and older. The law stripped me of all power as a parent seeking to protect my child. All three fields—education, counseling, and medicine—need to rethink how they handle not only their trans clients but also the people around them. Right now there are limited services for parents like myself.

It's hard to see a path when other families embrace your trans son's decisions and never once call or ask what you, the mother, think.

Donald had facial hair by age eighteen.

Donald's voice went tinny, then deep, so I saved J.'s voice on my answering machine.

She, she, she became he, he, he.

Right now, after many years of reflection and hard work, I dodge all pronouns as much as possible when referring to Donald in conversation. A linguistics professor at my university noticed I have developed a verbal tic when referring to my trans son. I tend to say "my Donnie" instead of "my son."

Donald is in New York. Donald is working hard. I am so proud of all that my Donald is doing.

Not he. Not she. Just, my Donald.

After reading the essays he wrote for this book, I am almost embarrassed by my reticence to call him my son, but some residual sense of loss about my daughter makes it difficult, even though I've come so much further in terms of accepting what Donald wants and deserves.

Donald, my son.

Gender Roles

What was more important to me in my role as a mother: to protect J. from being dismantled step by step, or to empower Donald to emerge with a new identity as a trans man?

In an effort to remain true to myself as a single mother of an only child, I could not willingly go along with completely erasing J. The biological father walked when I was still pregnant; the stepfather, whom I divorced when Donald was thirteen, manages to see him once or twice a year. There are no siblings.

Just me and J.

A family.

Two females.

One mother and one daughter.

All the various factors in my personal life led me to a career and financial situation more commonly associated with a man. I took charge of everything, bought my own house, excelled at work, and was continually promoted to ever more demanding jobs. When I first moved from the South to New England after my divorce, I actually wrangled with my future employer over my starting salary. Later, I learned from a top administrator that I was the only woman she had ever met who had done that. In her experience, only men had the gumption to press for more cash before they even started a job.

With no child support or life partner to help me, I had to become ever more gender neutral in how I lived my life to care for my young daughter.

But as J. transformed into Donald, everything flipped. I found myself shifting into ever more traditional feminine roles. I wanted to go to the mother-daughter tea at the high school, but Donald declined; I wanted Donald to wear a white dress to the high school graduation like all the other young women, but he arrived in a suit and tie. I used food to help heal the wounds that kept opening between us, making sure I prepared fine meals, like fresh swordfish and homemade mashed potatoes, for Donald so we'd eat together and talk about the things we both love—reading, writing, art, humor—rather than fall into our excruciating disagreements.

Donald became much more assertive about shaping his own life and secured internships he never would have aspired to as a young woman. As J., my child feared talking to cashiers when buying a bagel, but as Donald he lived on his own in New York City before even graduating college and plunged into the high-octane world of TV production. He's bluntly admitted to me that life in the United States is easier and much more fun living as a man.

He feels nature pulled a nasty trick and put him in the wrong body, and he's working to adjust that. I feel nature gave me a daughter and then, unexpectedly, took her away.

Both of those feelings and impressions are true and authentic.

I do not need to be a woman, and Donald does not have to be a man, to understand the agony inherent in that conundrum.

We just want to find a way to be humane to each other.

Endings and Beginnings

✦ ✦ ✦

Mapping Modern Grief

Mary Collins

"I am transgender," my teenaged daughter, J., says, her green eyes squinting with anxiety.

"Trans?" I ask. "What's that?"

I am still thinking about mundane things, like the dirty dishes on the counter. We sit at my favorite place in the house, the round kitchen table by a window with lacy curtains, where I drink tea and read my newspaper every morning.

"*Trans*, Mom. I am a man trapped in a woman's body."

The summer day's simmering breath coming through the screen suddenly feels like a panting animal.

"What?"

✦ ✦ ✦

My first fully modern loss.

It does not feel the same as when my father died when I was age fourteen.

It does not feel the same as when the love of my life left me when I was in my twenties.

In that moment at the kitchen table, I experienced a loss only made possible by our current culture, which allows—even empowers—a teenager to take steroids and have "top surgery" (trans speak for a double mastectomy) all before age twenty so his gender can match his person.

When J. legally changed her name to Donald and insisted we use male pronouns to refer to him, I resisted for a short time, but eventually gave up on "she," "her," and the entire idea that I have a daughter at all.

But when I said I thought Donald was moving too fast with his physical transition, the counselors, school advisors, and medical professionals told me I must face the inevitable.

When I said I was sad about the unique obstacles my child will have to deal with in the larger world as an adult, they told me to tamp down my homophobia and trans bias. Seek counseling to overcome your prejudices, they advised.

I am not ashamed or biased, I told them.

I am grieving the loss of my daughter, and that does not mean I do not love my trans son.

Modern loss. Modern grief.

None of them grasped any of it, so I share a story with one of the school advisors.

When the school had a mother-daughter tea for Mother's Day, Donald and I did not go, and skipped over to a nondescript Dunkin' Donuts in a strip mall instead. As we finished our iced coffees, both milky-white with extra cream, I noticed two guys with heavily tattooed arms sitting two tables away listening as we chatted about Cher's trans son, Chaz, who had been in the news a lot.

The men's shoulders seemed tight, their lips closed.

I eyed the pickup truck outside.

I stared at the ice cubes in my cheap plastic cup.

I told Donald we needed to leave.

He thought it was because I'd finished my drink.

In that moment I did not feel shame, I tell the advisor, just fear.

I take no issue with any individual's right to affirm and assert his or her identity.

But I know that outside the super-accommodating world of my child's liberal school, approximately 40 percent of Americans still disapprove of homosexuality. Imagine how they must perceive someone who is transgender? Even within the LGBTQ community, the T falls toward the end of the continuum.

In that moment, I explain to the advisor, I understood my daughter would never return. Her *person* remains, but my trans son faces a day-to-day life I never imagined for my child. As I drove Donald back to school, my fear transformed into something else, something that now follows me through my days, something I can only describe as grief.

I know from reading books and articles about parents with children who do not fall within "normal" parameters, in particular Andrew Solomon's book *Far from the Tree: Parents, Children, and the Search for Identity*, that millions of families struggle with this unusual form of grieving. Two tall parents might have a dwarf; a scholar might have an autistic boy who does not speak. Counselors focus on "acceptance" of the situation rather than processing the grief first, which, unfortunately, falls right in line with the American Psychiatric Association's recent decision to identify depression associated with deep grief as mental illness, not a natural reaction that an individual should be encouraged to feel and move through without guilt or shame. Leave it to American culture to take a fundamental human emotion and classify it as a condition.

I reflected on how I handled my father's death to help me cope with my situation with my trans son, but that only brought back memories of how poorly American culture handles even this most timeless of losses.

All I remember of the moment when I first heard my father had died were the white walls of my small bedroom, my mother by my bedside shaking from the stress of what she had to tell me, the sense of dislocation I felt when she spoke the news. I remember wrapping the cotton bedspread around my shoulders and leaning into the softness and warmth. I don't remember leaving the room or going downstairs or how I told my friends. I now associate white, not black, with death, and have purple, lilac, deep blue, yellow, and other colors on the walls in my house, but not white.

The general world treated my loss as sad, unfortunate, but nothing so out of the ordinary that I wasn't expected to return to school, to sports teams, to my student work job at my high school within the week. We had a church service, a burial; I missed a few days of classes and that was it.

Only now, as an adult researching grief and loss, have I discovered that just 4 percent of children in the United States under age fifteen lose a parent. When I asked my sister to guess the percentage (and she's a health-care professional), she said about 25 percent. In places and time periods in which such losses were more commonplace, the larger society was better equipped to recognize grief and loss as an ongoing experience—not something with concrete stages that you go through in lockstep, but something you carry with you, often always.

In American culture we do not celebrate a Day of the Dead, as they do in Mexico; we don't have secular altars in public spaces to honor those who have passed, as in many Eastern cultures. Here grief is more of an individual responsibility, a framework that encourages isolation and often morphs into debilitating depression. The fact that modern American life continues to add ever more complex types of loss just exacerbates the problem.

My emotional journey with Donald seems to more closely mirror more nebulous losses, such as moving away from someone I will never see again. The average American moves twelve times in his or her lifetime, and one in five children eventually move far away from their families, a geographic mortality rate, for want of a better term, that's startling when you consider that for most of human history, the majority of people rarely traveled more than fifty miles from where they grew up.

Similarly, a single woman like me with a decent job can have dozens of romantic relationships over a lifetime, a tremendous freedom that comes with a price: you become intimate with a much larger pool of people, but, conversely, you also experience the loss of that intimacy anew each time it doesn't work out.

I call that "good-bye grief."

When Donald came home after the top surgery, he felt freed of the physical binds he had used to compress his breasts for years. He could wear a light t-shirt with nothing on underneath on a hot July day. His shoulders sprang back when he walked now, instead of slouched. He held his head differently, more confidently, and looked outward instead of downward. He felt more at home in his own body.

I looked at his now slim torso and saw a fawn before me—all legs, reddish-brown coat, and so vulnerable I wanted to hire a bodyguard for him.

Donald's radical adjustment has made it easier for me to remember to use male pronouns when referring to him; I only slip up when I am out of Donald's presence and around strangers who ask about my family. At one point, while Donald was still in college, a contractor building a porch for me wanted to know if I had children. Without thinking, I said, yes, I have a daughter who is a sophomore in college.

Two weeks later Donald came home, and as we pulled into the driveway the contractor stuck his head in my car to say hello.

"Oh," he remarked later, "so you have two kids."

Oh.

I had no vocabulary to explain the complexity of my situation in such quick passing conversations.

Instead, despite taking great pride in being an honest and direct person, I say little and am left with what I wryly call my own grief geography, territory that no one else can navigate or fully know. Of course our ancient ancestors had their own grief maps as well, terra incognita to us now. Which leaves me with the timeless question: Why did we evolve to grieve? It leaves us despondent, lethargic, and plagued by headaches and stomachaches; none of these things are sexy or enhance our ability to interact with others. The trauma is so great that stress hormones can literally cause the heart to enlarge temporarily. Research in evolutionary biology proves that even though we don't want to experience this emotion, we can't be fully mature without it.

At a physical level, our faces cannot fake either happiness or sadness. When a person forms a sincere smile, they engage the muscles around the eyes that lead to crow's feet. You cannot fake that motion in the face.

There is also a sincere grief muscle, the corrugator muscle, which pulls together the eyebrows and wrinkles the forehead.

At a deep biological level we evolved to know for *certain* if someone is truly happy or sad.

At a deep biological level our entire body systems are programmed to handle losses, to allow emotions to vent and wax and wane as we recover. Indeed, most emotions only last seconds and rarely last more than hours.

I must acknowledge that at a fundamental level I actually gained some benefits from losing a parent young. I turned inward, rethought assumptions, felt less entitled, developed more empathy, paid closer attention to other people with sorrow, and emerged with a new identity, one infinitely more layered than the self-absorbed athlete I had been.

And as a teenager, I had listened to my father. I took his advice. And when he was gone, I had his words, and I did not challenge them.

"Be sure to love your work. Be good citizens and enjoy what life can offer. It can be a lot of fun if you let it," he advised in a handwritten letter in pale blue ink that now hangs in my study. "Remember me and the good times that we had and don't dwell on the sorrowful aspects of life."

I turned down law school and became a writer and a professor of creative writing, in part, because he empowered me with these words and with his early death.

Love your work. Be a good citizen.

I have never admitted that I benefitted in any way from experiencing such a deep loss at such a young age because I've somehow felt it inappropriate to express such conflicted feelings. In America, you're either grieving the loss of someone or you're "over" it.

I either love my trans son or I don't.

How do we do a better job of breaking free of such rigid thinking so we can accept a much wider range of griefs (yes, I am making that word up) as we face an ever evolving range of losses in modern life?

Step one: Get over the shame.

When I first started working on this essay, I felt so self-conscious writing about grief and loss for an American audience that I labeled the story file "G-Stories," so anyone walking in and out of my office area would not pepper me with questions about what I was writing. I feared they would think I was sad (I was not) or depressed (I was not), otherwise how else could I explain focusing my precious writing hours on such a topic?

At least one of my distant relatives lacked such inhibitions.

While clearing out an estate for an aunt on my father's side, my family came across some handwritten letters in a cloth bag hidden behind a picture frame. The time line at the top of one of the first pages read *Clonmel, Ireland, November 12th 1871.* My great-grandmother's father was sending news from the home country to his daughters in America. He wrote of church yard sales, the death of his son, and his longing and sadness because he knew he'd never again see the children who had sailed across the Atlantic. Now that the son who stayed in Ireland was gone, "we are left lonesome," John Sheedy wrote. "We have neither son nor daughter to call on when we have need of them. The grave and America left us a lone couple in Our Old Days."

His grief, hidden behind a frame for decades, came fully into my heart as I read his careful penmanship. At first, all I could think of was the Catholic knack for laying on the guilt, but then I also saw that by simply writing, by putting his true feelings to paper and sending it across the ocean for his daughters to feel, he'd let go of shame about his situation.

I am sad. I am lonely. I am full of grief because you are gone and your brother has died.

Clearly his daughters shared their father's pain, and perhaps even felt motivated by it to do the best they could in America, so that all the loss would result in true gains: good jobs, a good education, and a better world for their own children and grandchildren.

I cannot say these things for certain, but they did save the letters.

Now, John Sheedy's great-great-great granddaughter has become a grandson. The girl I set sail into the world came back across the water a different gender. Like John, I know my daughter will never return. Like John, I have put my various griefs in a bag and hid them behind a proverbial frame.

But the geography of my grief was terra incognita in his time.

Despite the counselor's advice, I pull it out now, like a map, with this essay, for all to see.

Birds of Spring

Donald Collins

"D'you want to change?"
"It's the only evidence of life."
—Evelyn Waugh, *Brideshead Revisited*

I have a tattoo of a robin on my left bicep, a medium-sized traditional piece, and my first. Tattoos became a part of my ever evolving vision of self sometime during my junior year of college. When I was working a paid internship in New York and had extra cash on hand, I found a reputable artist and started decorating.

I prepare to tell my mother about this tattoo as we depart from a local coffee shop. I'm waiting for the magic moment between the car's air conditioning *really* working and us reversing out of the parking spot.

So many long, difficult talks between my mother and me have taken place in a car. I remember her visiting me at boarding school, taking me for a much-needed lunch and a drive. We would park somewhere and talk at length in our seats. She would ask questions with the kind of frustration that comes from knowing that someone is unhappy and not knowing how to help that person. I would desperately try to impart any understanding of the unhappiness I had no name for. Then, with something short of relief, she would return home and I, to school.

Today we are both in good spirits, and I am hesitant to stir up any trouble. But the opportune moment lingers and luckily, I've paved my own way. These hundred difficult talks of ours, some harder than others, make my admission near casual.

"I got a tattoo in New York," I tell her. "I thought about it for a long time, and I'm very happy with it. I just didn't want to surprise you."

I show her the tattoo, and she *is* surprised, but polite.

"It's very well done," she remarks.

After getting the tattoo, I found out the robin is the state bird of Connecticut—site of my coming out, my boarding school years, and my family's current home. I chose it because robins are, mythically, the bird of springtime, of new beginnings. Its seasonal arrival heralds the budding of trees, warmer weather, and migrations.

Being trans, or *my* way of being trans, involves a lot of starting over. I filled out hours of paperwork to create this person. I celebrate new birthdays and anniversaries for myself. I have a new name, a new body, and a new will to enjoy life. Opportunities and friendships ripen around the arrival of this new person. He is welcome, more than welcome, in this long-hibernating world of his own making.

I wear my robin like a badge and bring my own spring with me.

✦ ✦ ✦

While I was experiencing this spring-of-myself, my mother grieved for her daughter of seasons past.

Parents and guardians often experience a profound sense of loss when a child articulates a trans or gender-variant identity. In their handbook *The Transgender Child*, Stephanie Brill and Rachel Pepper divide this loss into two primary categories: grief over "lost dreams" and grief for "the child who goes away."

My mother grieved my symbolic feminine future and my literal feminine present. Her vision for my life became complicated, was rearranged, and fell out of focus, while I began to see things clearly for the first time.

✦ ✦ ✦

I had just started boarding high school at Loomis Chaffee when I intuited a severe misalignment between my physical and mental gender orientation. My parents had divorced in the months previous, and while Dad remained in Virginia, Mom and I moved from my hometown of Alexandria to her hometown of West Hartford, a Connecticut suburb.

I had only seen pictures of the house we moved to, a sweet but drafty colonial home a block from the town center.

Despite the pressures of starting her new teaching job, my mother was revitalized and clearly relieved to be away from the emotional toxicity of our previous home. It was my own childish protesting that had kept her from moving away a year earlier. But while my mom may have been ready for her new start, I wasn't ready for mine. I failed to connect with our new home. No end of painting and rearranging made my chilly (and now terribly painted) room comfortable. I took to sleeping in the TV room on a spare mattress.

Even though Loomis was within driving distance of our house, boarding was a more practical option. It meant my mom, being my primary parent, didn't have to stress about how I would get to school every day. It would give her some time to adjust to a demanding new position as a professor, and me a much-needed sense of community. My mom and all her siblings had gone to Loomis, and it was the only place she would allow me to board. It was also the only high school I applied to.

The school is still a relative baby among the New England prep elite, a class of expensive institutions including the hundred-years-older Andover, Exeter, Deerfield, and Miss Porter's. Perhaps its "youthful" 1874 founding contributes to Loomis's distinctly new-age vibe. We're just a little more chill, which by prep school standards isn't actually *that* chill.

Every morning began with signing in at breakfast and participating in a mandatory "work-job," a rotating chore that could be anything from trash pickup, busing dishes, or delivering papers. To leave campus on foot you had to sign out, and to leave in a car you had to get written permission from a faculty member or have a parent call ahead. Low-level misbehavior resulted in restrictions to campus, and upper-level conduct violations, called "Level Twos" (drinking, drugs, and wanton fornication), resulted in students having to complete "work hours" for the school. Overall, the system was benevolent, involving more red string than red tape—especially compared to our British counterparts—but still enough to stifle distracted seventeen-year-olds.

My first two years of Loomis went by in a melancholy blur. I

enjoyed my coursework, met a few close friends, but otherwise deteriorated quickly, slipping into intense periods of depression.

In eighth grade I had participated in hyper-feminine presentation,
complete with long hair, rings, scarves, and tailored clothing, believing it would help me fit it more and banking that I would adapt to it
with time. My mother encouraged my child-self to be active, confident,
and allowed me to dress in boyish clothes. But as I grew up, she and
the world around me gradually enforced the bodily reality of gendered
culture.

Girls don't wear boys' clothes.

This is gender socialization, a set of codes, stereotypes, and expectations relentlessly baked in until they become the norm.

My "girl" clothes caused me great discomfort, but everything was
easier when I wore them. People didn't correct my behavior or appearance. I didn't stand out. But though the long hair, rings, scarves and
tailored clothing helped me fit in, by the end of my freshman year, I
packed everything away, feeling suffocated. Girls' clothes were like the
sweaty trappings of a theater costume, right for the part I was playing
but not for me. Within months of being at Loomis, I cut my hair slop-
pily short and took to wearing oversized thrift-store men's clothing. I
became less and less recognizable to my mother. My dad wondered if
I was gay. Friends struggled to interpret my behavior. I was talkative,
cheerful—then suddenly morose, beyond reach.

"You wear that sweater every day," my friend Sus joked one
morning.

"Cut it out," I snapped at her. "Don't make fun of how I dress."

I had weekly sessions with Kendall, an agreeable, grounded therapist, for over two years. She was the first adult I expressed my gender
dissonance to. Kendall was one of several mental health practitioners
who visited Loomis weekly to conduct on-site appointments. Despite
not being technically classified as a "gender therapist," she became my
tether to a kind of gender-enlightened sensibility. I can still visualize
us sitting opposite each other in the scratchy chairs of Loomis's health
center attic. The stuffy, cream-colored infirmary suggested, and still

does, that Red Cross nurses would burst in any moment with news of an armistice.

"Sometimes," I told her, "I feel like my life would have been so much better if I were a boy."

Being the soft-spoken professional she was, Kendall never steered our sessions, though she may have been long aware of the dissatisfaction *I* couldn't pin down. She provided me a space to sort and categorize my own thoughts, to express feelings I had long repressed and devalued. I didn't know my "life" as a boy was possible until I started talking about it, until I started *needing* it to be possible.

I don't understand the hard-and-fast "therapy doesn't work" mindset, because therapy is an individual process and experience. It worked for *me*. It indulged my hopeless self-obsession and allowed me to revisit the sites of my shame and interrogate their meanings. It helped me feel less angry, less damaged. It put me in control of my own betterment. After my "coming out" session with Kendall I took the time to lie quietly in my room and explore the shocking (at the time) words I had spoken.

During our next appointment I got specific: "I think I'm transgender."

✦ ✦ ✦

On a winter weekend home from school my senior year, I very emotionally told my mother these exact words in our kitchen. I noticed a blank expression in her eyes. I should have known in that moment that the word did not make contact with her. She didn't understand. She reassured me that things were going to be okay and thanked me for telling her. Emboldened by this response, I began to elaborate on my plans (whoops!). I was changing my name and pronouns at school and would begin living "as a man" full time immediately. Then I saw the word connect, and the mood changed.

"*What?*" she said, incredulous.

By the end of the evening we were both exhausted from crying and arguing. I felt deeply offended that I'd had to endure a Socratic discourse to get permission to be myself at school (I was taking Intro to Philosophy at the time). I also felt deeply disheartened about my progress with this new, seemingly insurmountable roadblock in my way. Not only was my mom forbidding me to come out; she was devastated by my choice.

My mother would later explain to me that her conception of "trans" informed her confused reaction, because she believed it signified identification with both male and female traits, understandable considering that the word *trans* comes from the Latin root for "across" or "beyond." Indeed, many trans people do identify with both male and female genders (also with more genders and no genders). But to my mom's mind, the identification was milder. I was a "girl" who felt a little like a "boy" sometimes. This was fine with her as long as it didn't involve me changing any part of myself. Not surprisingly, that didn't work for me at all.

She asked me not to come out at school, to put it off, to give us some time to think all this through. I've never been one to disobey my mom or my family, but her request was directly at odds with my sense of well-being.

"Don't do this," my mother said.

✦ ✦ ✦

I came out at the Christmas party of my (almost) all-girls dorm a week later.

"We have a short announcement before the party ends," my dorm parent Mrs. A. shouted into the giggling crowd. Everyone quieted, and she gestured for me to speak.

I scratched nervously at the back of my neck, itchy from a new haircut earlier in the day. My red mop top was now carved into a ridiculous faux-hawk, one of the few choices I can honestly say my mom was right in protesting.

"I have something important I want to tell you," I said to the room of attentive girls, standing amid streamers and tables of cupcakes. My words were clumsy, a second test flight hot on the heels of my first coming-out disaster.

"I identify as transgender," I continued slowly. "I feel like a boy, even though I was born a girl. Everyone here knows me as 'J.,' but I would prefer to go by the name 'Donnie' and male pronouns."

✦   ✦   ✦

In my senior year of college, more than four years after coming out at Loomis, I was a guest speaker at a gender studies class. The class, taught by my favorite Emerson professor, had just completed their readings for the "transgender" unit. I functioned as a kind of primary source, an interactive exhibit.

The discussion veered toward my previously toxic feelings toward hegemonic (traditional, stereotypical) femininity. I found myself being honest with the class about my high school anger toward my "feminine" body and my earlier beliefs that masculinity was a superior, more desirable identity. For months, I told them, I even refrained from saying the word "cute" because it was "girly."

"How do you feel about women and girls now?" piped a student in the back.

Completely off guard, I began to cry.

"I love girls," I stammered. "Girls are amazing. Girls saved my life."

I told them about that night at the dorm, my first coming-out "audience," those forty girls who hugged me, supported me, and respected me. Girls who corrected their peers, checked in on me, remained some of my closest friends in the years to come. I fell asleep in the dorm that night hating every part of myself called "girl," and yet the whole time it was girls who had carried me toward myself.

Remembering my own devaluation of women and girls because the gender was forced upon me—and wasn't right for me—brings me great shame. My confrontations with these memories are difficult, but essential. I am finally able to express gratitude toward the women, including my mother and grandmother, who made *me* possible. I am finally able to treat the Loomis girls, those first allies of mine, with the same care and respect with which they treated me.

I continue to repair.

✦ ✦ ✦

As much as the support of Palmer Dormitory meant to me, it was not the same as the support of a parent. Indeed, there was nothing perfect about my coming-out in high school. I was asked invasive questions, I got called out in bathrooms, and I resented being four years into an all-girl living situation and sitting at all-girl tables during weekly "family style" dinners. But despite its feeble imperfections, Loomis was my home. Like many of its alumni, I hated it, and it saved me. But senior spring, as I strengthened my relationship with this school "family," my relationship with my mother reached new lows.

✦ ✦ ✦

My college counselor, Beatrice, called my mom at home with the answer to a simple admissions question. She used the name "Donnie" when referring to me. This is how my mother learned I had come out at school. And she didn't even like Beatrice to begin with.

"I had to find out from that . . . *woman!*" she hissed.

I wanted to remind my mom that she had already found out from *me.* I had told her first, and she could have been a part of this process. My mom needed more time, and I had no more time left to give.

I felt, to use an expression from *Psycho*'s Norman Bates (a terrible role model), deeply mired in my "private traps." My mother and I argued in circles, and for all of it, neither of us ever budged an inch.

Our late-night weekend living room conversations only served to put our views into sharper contrast: me, certain I needed legal and physical procedures to confirm my gender; she, distraught, convinced I was ruining my life. Loomis, unsure of how to manage its first out trans student, reacted in earnest accommodation. When it became clear that my mom had not offered a Christmas Party Welcome, they froze communication. My mother, who felt my gender presentation at school was a family affair, was appalled at being "iced out" and never consulted. Because she and her siblings had gone to Loomis, she felt my behavior could negatively impact the entire Collins family and their relationship with the school.

✦ ✦ ✦

I took refuge in my social renaissance. While my early Loomis years were marred with reclusion and anxiety, senior year I found endless possibilities in the fledgling confidence coming out had given me. For nearly four years, my oddball presentation and palpable unhappiness had stymied my peers. But now, as my friend Sus put it, things began to "make sense" to them. I made new friends, spent more time with older ones, and actually began to enjoy myself. I cherished the majority support of the student body, but at the time didn't realize how anomalous it was.

According to their 2011 study, the National Center for Transgender Equality reported 82 percent of trans youth feel unsafe at school. More than half of these respondents admitted to skipping school on a regular basis to avoid bullying.

When many of my high school friends came out as gay, bi, or trans in college, I realized that self-pitying perceptions of my own rareness were overstated. *I* came out in high school, but so many others didn't or couldn't.

✦ ✦ ✦

The only thing that remained stagnant amid my final lap was the unrelenting tension between my mother and me. Loomis, the one-time source of all my stress and exhaustion, was now my haven. My mom, my truest confidant and advocate, was now part opposition, part victim. I was finally accomplishing everything she had hoped for me— genuine optimism for myself, interesting classwork, a thriving social life—but it all came at the expense of her "daughter," the one price she was *not* willing to pay.

When I graduated Loomis, the purgatorial haze remained.

✦ ✦ ✦

I had been granted "permission" to graduate in the masculine style, khakis and a blue blazer with a flower, coincidentally, the pledge uniform of my college fraternity. Students grouped together in common rooms, chatting and getting ready as their families parked. We eventually convened on the quadrangle, a big green lawn dwarfed by trees and cut into four parts by a clay path. There, after much mingling and tearfulness, the genders were split into their two lines and herded onto bleachers. Our delirious, pomaded heads smiled for the camera and then filed through the main academic hall.

In a yard facing the picturesque entrance road, the senior class found the chairs we would call home for the next four hours. I brimmed with accomplishment and something else . . . disappointment?

After six months as "Donnie," I would be graduating under my birth name, "J."

My family had financed my education in conjunction with academic scholarships, and this was their official request. Actually, I don't fully know *what* their request was. Maybe my mother's nostalgic wish or her last bid to have "J." leave Loomis "alive." It stung and, ultimately, was a shoddy compromise.

My part of the roll call only lasted a few seconds. I stepped on stage in my blazer and khakis to the cheers of my classmates. The juxtaposition of the distinctly masculine clothes and the feminine name created a strange space. It wasn't what I wanted; it wasn't what my mom wanted. But the ceremony moved forward. And with a cloudless sky above and the prospect of lunch ahead, the class of 2011 tossed their proverbial caps in the air (we had no caps).

I was overwhelmed with bittersweet feelings. I said good-bye to friends and mentors, and savored quiet last moments in places I'd called home. These relationships stayed with me on my journey, and I am infinitely better off for having loved and hated that school.

I remember my family, my mother, eyes filled with pride for the symbolic occasion.

The child graduates high school.

I was going away, further away from them. I was leaving Loomis, and in a stranger, truer sense, I was leaving my family.

Privately, later that day, someone from the registrar's office handed me another diploma, one bearing my chosen name. It felt like contraband.

✦ ✦ ✦

If I seem callous or cold-hearted toward my mom, know that some-times I am. When the people we love hurt us, often these are the only behaviors we find strength in. I continued to "live my truth," knowing that my mother was grieving and in pain because I needed to survive.

Going into college, I couldn't cope with my mom's attachment to the very things I hated most about myself. Just as I needed to feel some space to change what wasn't working for me, I felt more trapped by her devotion to J., her only child, her only *daughter*.

J. is both real and unreal; she existed, she is me, and yet she is not who I *am*. To look through our house, one would think I have a sister. For a while my mother continued to display photos of me before I was, as Laverne Cox says, my "authentic self." On low shelves and storage cabinets sat these photos of a slim, smiling girl with long red hair. She would seem happy if I didn't know her so well.

During my next four years after Loomis, I continued to start over. For months, my mother and I didn't speak, and for many more, we continued to clash over increasingly high stakes.

I met wonderful people during my time in Boston and then New York, called them *friends* and *family*. I felt hopeless, undertook exhaust-ing projects, sought help, and practiced caring for my mind and body in new ways. I reveled in sharing life-changing words and ideas. I actively created my own identity, contributed to my own history, and even tried to lend some of my experience to others.

Amid everything, I wondered when, and if, my mom and I would have our own spring. I wondered if we could begin again.

Sharing Our Story
with Others

✦ ✦ ✦

Coming out is a phrase associated with the LGBTQ community that describes the outward expression of an internal identification. *Coming out of the closet* suggests that this identification brings you from a place of repression and hiding to a place of ownership and openness. *She just came out as a lesbian. He finally came out to his parents.*

In her 2013 article in *Mental Floss*, Arika Okrent ties the phrase's origin to New York's infamous gay and drag "debutante balls." Coming out, she writes, "did not refer to coming out of hiding, but to joining into a society of peers."

Closeted is a term for someone who never comes out, who has an internal LGBTQ identification not expressed publicly.

Being *outed* is when someone else wrongly forces the moment of coming-out upon you.

Donald Has Something
He Would Like to Tell the Class

Donald Collins

> How to explain, in a culture frantic for resolution,
> that sometimes the shit stays messy?
> —Maggie Nelson, *The Argonauts*

My first major coming-out happened when I stood up at my dorm's Christmas party and said, "I'm trans." It also happened when I spoke to my mother in our kitchen. And it happened again when I finally created a Facebook at seventeen.

Much like R. Kelly's infamous thirty-three-chapter opera *Trapped in the Closet*, coming out is a process, with exhausting ups and downs, that continues to happen relentlessly.

✦ ✦ ✦

Non-trans people sometimes express a strain of entitlement that goes something like this: "I deserve to know if anyone I meet is transgender." I'm trans. Being trans is a part of my identity. I'm also a writer, an amateur painter, and the proud owner of a used Ford Focus. The compulsion to "know" I'm trans wrongly assumes that this information is necessary for others to have, when most of the time it's not. The compulsion to "know" also propagates the idea that trans people are hiding something, that we are frauds or illusionists, that we are not *real*. Our gender is unfairly treated as if it were a costume that we must admit to wearing.

In her 1990 book, *Gender Trouble*, theorist Judith Butler famously asserted that gender identity is characterized by "a stylized repetition of acts through time." This is gender performativity theory, the idea that gender is a kind of behavioral consistency both in and of a system.

Butler herself was quick to point out that this doesn't mean we all have the empowering ability to constantly change our gender depending on what clothes we put on in the morning. As Sarah Salih explains in her essay on Butler, our "choices" surrounding our gender exist within a "regulatory frame." Rather than artists with infinite supplies, daily creating new and exciting works of gender, we're kind of stuck with paint-by-numbers.

Many scholars and thinkers have expanded on Butler's theory or challenged other, more rudimentary "performance" based theories. Julia Serano recalls her own experiences as a trans woman in doing so, asserting, "Many of us who have physically transitioned from one sex to the other understand that our perceived gender is typically not a product of our 'performance' (i.e., gender expression/gender roles) but rather our physical appearance (in particular, our secondary sex characteristics)."

If you do not fit easily into a visual gender category, you are complicating someone's constant categorization of all nearby bodies. You are challenging the entire system of gender on which the viewer's identity is built. Oftentimes, onlookers may seek to fix this processing glitch by avoiding ("Don't stare, honey"), clarifying ("Are you a boy or a girl?"), or accosting ("What are *you* doing in this bathroom?"). They might just burn you with their laser eyes.

It's important to establish the weight of both sides when it comes to the compulsion to "know" and the decision to share. On one side, we have curiosity; on the other, we have a potential minefield. Many, if not most, trans people do not get to opt out of the minefield.

Coming-out scratches a variety of itches. It can be a personal deliverance or a medical or clerical necessity. The following are situations when I came out for one reason or another:

Coming out to a café cashier at a bus station to explain why the name on my credit card doesn't match my appearance.

Coming out to the bus driver a few minutes later to explain the same thing about my license.

Coming out to my tattooist, because I really liked her and it seemed chill.

Coming out to a new doctor in Hartford, Connecticut, and again when I move to Los Angeles.

Coming out at a party to the friend of a friend, whose own sibling is gender variant and who had some questions for me.

Coming out at two Departments of Motor Vehicles in one day trying to (unsuccessfully) get one of them to change my gender marker from "F" to "M."

Coming out in an essay to write about coming out.

There are many days when I don't come out to anyone. I just live my life, and some of the people in it know I'm trans and others don't. A lot of the time, sharing the fact that I'm trans is something I do to establish that I trust someone and want to know them better. Being "stealth" means I have to censor my stories, my history, and my stresses. I can most fully be myself by including "trans."

I'll admit that I often hate the moment when I tell people. I *feel* them look at me differently. I *feel* them explaining my behavior with this new information, or at least I *think* I feel it. I imagine them scrutinizing my body, my voice, even my hobbies. *Oh, that's why Donald bakes so much—he was raised as a girl!* I've had people tell me I have "women's hands" and that I stretch better after a workout because "women are more flexible."

Gender is a system maintained by a ruthless neighborhood watch (us). We constantly judge and disparage other people's bodies, both in and out of gender contexts. *Are they too fat? Are they too thin? Are they short? Do they have acne? Is it severe? Are they bald? Are their boobs too big or small?* I do it all the time in my own head, with the goal of not letting these runaway thoughts get legitimized by speaking them or acting on them. It's hard not to be obsessed with other people's bodies when you spend so much time obsessed with your own. And maybe that's why I sometimes hate that moment after I come out because it makes me feel so self-conscious about my own body and about the way I look at other people's.

✦   ✦   ✦

My coming out: part two (the reckoning) happened my junior year of college. I pledged a fraternity called Phi Alpha Tau, came out as trans on cable news, and ultimately found myself in possession of $23,000. I'll start at the beginning.

By the fall of my junior year, I had been on testosterone for almost three years, my name was legally changed, and I lived in my own room on campus as an RA. My mother and I were on decent terms but shaky ground. She knew I was pursuing top surgery to flatten my chest, another physical alteration she couldn't get behind. I proceeded in the planning stage without her. We were both completely emotionally exhausted; I tried to just keep my own shit together and keep it far from her door.

I like to think of my experience joining Phi Alpha Tau as some kind of daytime movie special. It's a feel-good story; it's a cautionary tale; it's a melodrama and a buddy comedy.

Tau (pronounced "Tah") is a single-chapter fraternity dedicated to the "communicative arts," which includes film, TV, journalism, theater, music, marketing, and writing. Emerson College, thankfully, has no frat houses, so Tau's sense of community operates on the organization and commitment of its brothers alone. When I joined, our membership was around thirty.

I had never considered joining a fraternity before entering college, and I still can't fully comprehend I'm *in* a fraternity. Most people I meet can't either. They ask, "What *kind* of fraternity?"

My roommate pledged Tau his sophomore year. I became enamored with his new "brothers," realizing that many students I admired on campus were also members. A friend and I went out for Tau the following winter. We submitted letters and resumes, were interviewed casually by individual brothers, and then attended a "smoker," a more formal interview process with the majority of the active brotherhood.

Fraternities are fundamentally exclusive organizations. They accept the people they want and turn away those they don't. At any college, especially a smallish one like Emerson, this rejection, however politely worded, hurts. Everyone knows if someone didn't get a "bid," the term that describes whether a fraternity wants you or not.

Tau is inclusive of a variety of personalities: hard partiers, quiet scholars, dedicated entrepreneurs, and brilliant performers. It's also known for being gay friendly, and when I sought entry, already had one trans member. But like any fraternity, Tau turns people away. To this day, my personal experience of unconditional support from the fraternity clashes with its status as an ultimately exclusive, conditional organization.

My motives for joining Tau were actually a jumble of contradictions. Fraternity life first appealed to me because it was separate from my "trans" life. It was a place where I could socialize like the extroverted college kid I wished I was and meet people from all different majors. Yet it was also a place where an only child and a trans guy could be called "brother." I needed validation *as a boy*, and it felt great when that validation came *from other boys*. I craved the feverish declarations of this family. That we all loved each other, that our homes were always open to each other, that we were available at all hours for brothers who needed us.

My mom and I still kept up a tentative correspondence. When I informed her I was pledging, she was surprised but supportive once I told her more about the fraternity. She always encouraged me to expand my social comfort zone and knew I would benefit from the kind of brotherly support Tau could offer.

My friend and I gratefully received and accepted bids. Our pledge class of ten convened a night later to begin the "new member process," a two-week, highly secretive ordeal. Fraternity members joke that pledging is "the most fun you don't want to have again." I will clarify that though I was not *always* having fun during this period, I was *never* hazed.

While pledging, we wore khakis, a collared shirt with tie, a blue blazer, and a fresh white carnation during "business hours" and evening meetings. For me, the most taxing part of it was the sheer amount of clothing layers I had to wear. I was still planning my top surgery and wearing binders to flatten my chest.

About a week into the process I received some bad news on this exact issue. My insurance claim for the surgery, a veritable thesis of paperwork, including proof of my name change, hormone therapy, and official letters of support from a counselor and endocrinologist, was denied.

✦ ✦ ✦

Many doctors' offices that offer gender-confirming surgical procedures don't even entertain insurance claims because, historically, it's pretty futile. Only recently are tides turning. Since being "trans" is something that still has to be "diagnosed" to be legitimate in the eyes of insurers, it's frustrating when medical-care systems won't actually provide *care* for the diagnosis they force on you. It's beyond frustrating; it's a kind of demolition.

My doctor's office *did* work with insurance, and when it called to tell me the claim was denied, I was devastated. I was also shopping for neckties in an H&M, and so I hurried outside to cry on the curb. My pledge brother Alex reassured me, and we plodded slowly back to campus.

The sweat pooling on my back and ribs under all my layers of clothing stung with each step. I had been doing so well, trusting that all my discomfort would be over soon. Yet every day I had believed myself closer to top surgery, my rejected claim was sitting in a clerk's outbox. I possessed some savings, but out of pocket, the surgery was going to cost more than $8,000. I didn't have $8,000.

✦ ✦ ✦

A few months earlier, I switched from my mother's insurance to my school's. She and I had both agreed to the terms. My mom didn't feel comfortable having her insurance cover the physical changes she was opposed to, and by having me move policies, we were able to remove at least one point of conflict from the list.

My school's policy covered hormone treatment, but its attitude toward GCS was vague. Emerson's health-center director was tireless in helping me, and together we pored over the policy to find some way to appeal.

I couldn't *really* share my claim defeat with my mother because I thought it might be a kind of victory to her—not that I was sad about it but because the medical system was preventing the same thing *she* wanted to prevent.

I missed my mom, who as a single parent and often self-employed writer/editor always had a kind of doggedness and resourcefulness in dealing with bureaucracy. She knows where to apply pressure and never forgets to follow up. Indeed, no matter how hard I tried to keep my "shit" from her door, there were days when I broke down and called her. I needed a ride somewhere or I needed help with a bill or I was just really depressed. These calls were our white flags, proof that our bond was intact.

My fraternity brothers were attentive and kind, but they were peers, not parents. It just so happened they were high-functioning peers. The insurance-claim debacle prompted me to come out to my pledge class, many of who did not know I was transgender. One of my pledge brothers, Dave, exhibited his characteristic gentility.

"I have no idea what that means," he told me earnestly. "Tell me about it."

I told them about it. The situation made its way to our pledgemaster (he who runs pledge) and then the active brotherhood.

I had no idea how far the information had carried. But by the meeting later that night, they had promised to help fund-raise so I could afford top surgery.

I graciously thanked them. *They're really nice*, I thought, *but who are they kidding?*

They certainly weren't kidding me. A central core of brothers set up a page and worked tirelessly to fund-raise toward the cost of my surgery. Within twenty-four hours they had almost $2,000.

Another of my brothers, Ben, a journalist worked for *Out* magazine at the time, conducted a short interview with me in response to the campaign. "Boston Fraternity Raises Money for Trans Brother" read the headline of the article.

Within another twenty-four hours, donations were pouring in from around the world.

I missed two days of work at my campus office job while I entertained media inquiries. Other RAs graciously covered my "on duty" nights at the dorm. I skipped some classes and fell asleep in others.

A national LGBTQ organization asked me to sign with them as a spokesperson. *Inside Edition* offered us $3,000 for our story if we would give them before-and-after pictures of me. Surgeons e-mailed me offering to do my surgery "free of cost." I said no to these, but agreed to other media inquiries. *HuffPost Live* had us on-air. We were on the front page of the *Boston Herald* and got a feature in the *Boston Globe* and a follow-up with *Out*.

Ours was the heartwarming story of the moment. We were rehabilitating the shattered respectability of fraternities, prompting an outpouring of love from "Greek" orgs and comments like "That's what a fraternity *should* be like." I was thrilled to bring such positive attention to my new brothers, and to the inconsistent state of trans health care. I was less clear about the attention directed toward my body and me.

On the first day of media, I called my mother to tell her firsthand what was happening. It was late. Next to me, my "big brother" Ryan mapped out a schedule to help me manage the next twenty-four hours. Homework, interview, food, interview, sleep, interview.

"You might see me on TV," I warned my mom.

Her voice was measured, brimming with concern for me, for herself. I can't remember our conversation, only a feeling. *Be careful.*

Like an outsize version of my coming-out at Loomis, this public stage represented a dramatic new step. I wasn't ready or willing to share everything. How could I talk about my family when things were still so muddy and difficult with them? How did I answer questions about my parent's reactions? How could I cast off my privacy but keep my mother's intact?

The answer was that I couldn't. But I didn't know it yet.

Within those first twenty-four hours, I wrote a thankful post about the fund-raiser update on my Tumblr. I was stunned when other trans people reblogged it and a vocal minority disparaged me. Why was my surgery "free" while they were working overtime for theirs? *Lucky bastard!*

Others were mad I wouldn't share the wealth, and strangers e-mailed me asking for the money. Even those who passed along messages of support occasionally sent terse follow-ups because I wasn't getting back to them fast enough. A student posted anonymously on a public Emerson "confessional" Facebook page, accusing me of using donations to buy coffee at Starbucks. Transphobic forums and articles surfaced in response to the expanding list of articles. I read comments from people who made light of killing and raping me and people like me. I occupied pages of Google web and image searches. There would be no going back. It was the fastest, most brutal education I have ever received.

On day two I answered a phone call from my mother, in distress. She was concerned about the questions I would receive going forward.

"They'll want to know about me," she said. "They're going to ask about your family and where we are in all this."

She asked me to shut it down, and I readily agreed.

The boys were fully supportive of my decision. After nearly three days in the media spotlight, we had raised $23,308. My surgery was scheduled for the winter break, only weeks away.

"We accomplished what we set out to do," my brother Christian said.

He was right. They had helped me; I had helped myself. We pledged

the excess funds to the Jim Collins Foundation (no relation), an organization that gives grants for gender-confirming surgeries to those in
need. A storybook ending.

✦ ✦ ✦

Within the next day or two, the insurance company "clarified" its position and agreed to cover my surgery.

My fraternity brothers and I all assumed this was a ploy to save face
after the punishing media coverage, but we were discouraged by the
college's PR department from publicly stating so. A few days later I was
told that a lost memo had been found proving Emerson's insurance to
be trans-inclusive. The policy had just never been updated correctly.
My surgery would be covered, and future trans students would be saved
the trouble of having to crowdsource their funds.

At first I was mortified. After all, we had just fund-raised $23,000
that I didn't actually need anymore. But then I realized: this is way better. We donated more than expected to the Jim Collins Foundation, and
my medical care was rightly in the hands of a medical-care provider.
Perhaps most importantly, this wouldn't happen again at Emerson.

On the home front, Mom and I both breathed easier, knowing *our*
problems were back safe with us.

Later still, I learned that, through all this, my stepfather Andrew
(who I call my dad because he took on that role) had made a series of
calls to the college asking them to investigate the issue. It was his calls
that prompted the paperwork search.

✦ ✦ ✦

By agreeing to come out, be visible, and share my story, I achieved so
much. My surgery was financed in full, the college's insurance policy
was clarified to benefit others, and all the money I didn't need was going to a worthy charity.

So why did I feel so much anger and shame?

I felt I had sold out myself by agreeing to be "trans" for the camera.
As much as I long to be social and fun, I'm also incredibly private. I

enjoy being alone for long periods of time. I've never had the compulsion to go to a club or even to Disneyland. But it wasn't the media overkill that upset me; it was the sneaking suspicion that I was more manipulative and desperate for help than I had realized. Once the fundraiser took off, I quickly understood that if I played "trans" in all the right ways, people would help me get what I needed. And they did.

I *do* feel like I didn't earn an all-expenses-paid surgery, even though I sweated so hard for my physical and mental health progress. I *do* feel guilty and embarrassed about all the attention. And I *do* feel shitty and ungrateful for not being solely positive about all the amazing help I received. I love my fraternity, and I love my brothers. I was so hurt when those few trans people termed me a lucky bastard, but that's *exactly what I am.*

Disclosure

Mary Collins

A woman in her sixties spills hot tea across my table in a bagel shop.

The conversation begins. Don't worry, I assure her.

We exchange simple introductions, then, for some reason, she asks the question: Do you have children?

Yes, a daughter, I say reflexively.

In the next millisecond I feel compromised, caught in some weird disclosure game I still haven't figured out how to navigate with integrity.

She has no children, she tells me.

Is my daughter in college?

Yes.

Then I shift the topic to bagels and the weather.

In the past I had a daughter, but now I have a transgender son. Just weeks prior to the spilt-tea incident, he (I use that pronoun with confidence at this point in the story) had a hysterectomy, the final step in his effort to make Donald's gender identity match his body. But in that random moment in that mundane space I was on autopilot, and in the primitive parts of my mind that allow me to speak without thinking, my daughter still resides.

After several years of practice, I know now not to weigh down the situation with the truth. I will not see that woman again. I do have a child. That child was in college at that time. I do not need to explain that I had a daughter but now have a son and they are one and the same person.

I am making up my own disclosure agreement as I go along, and I know that Donald has had to do the same.

In his case, now that he's had top surgery and takes hormones, he can more easily present as male anywhere he wants. Transgender people refer to this as going "stealth." When he worked in New York City as an intern for several organizations, his resume gave him away (if that's even the right phrase) a bit because of some guest-speaking assignments he listed on it. But his fellow interns never knew, even his housemates—five men in a jammed townhouse in Brooklyn—didn't know until he chose to tell them a week before he moved out.

Did it matter? Would anyone answer the woman in the bagel shop with phrases like "Yes, I have children, a daughter with cerebral palsy"? Or how about "Yes, I have a child, a gay son in college." So why do I feel deceptive when I say I have a daughter instead of saying I have a son? Why did I feel a touch of unease that Donald had not told his house-mates that he is a trans man?

I could have felt positive about his discretion, the yin to disclosure's yang. Why make people feel uncomfortable about something that's re-ally none of their business? It shouldn't impact the way they perceive you or treat you.

Donald himself has told me that there's nothing to "disclose," since that infers he has something to hide. While driving back from grab-bing an iced coffee together, he surprised me with his level of anger about people online comparing the case of Rachel Dolezal, the now former president of the NAACP chapter in Spokane, Washington, who is a white woman who pretended to be black, with Bruce Jenner coming out as Caitlyn.

Dolezal lied and deceived to further herself, Donald argued, but Jenner sought to finally tell the truth. My trans son flushed red and tensed his shoulders while summarizing the way people online dis-cussed parallels between the two stories. I told him to put his views in his essay, because I do not fully grasp his argument and hope I'll under-stand it better if he writes it down.

I do know that I'd be ashamed if I had a daughter who tried to pass as black and secured jobs and even college scholarships because of her ruse, but I am not ashamed that I have a transgender son. I am confused. I am afraid. I need to educate myself more about what that means for him. But I am awed by the fact that my child has the courage to engage in a journey toward self-realization that few people could ever think to undertake. I questioned physical steps he took at such an early age that even medical professionals argue about, but the feelings I have about that are not shame based.

When I look at the medical literature, with imposing titles like *Journal of Homosexuality*, about disclosure for anyone on the LGBTQ continuum, I hear conflicting messages.

Transgender people who *do not* disclose their status struggle more with depression and are more apt to harm themselves or even commit suicide.

Transgender people who *do* come out face a lot more harassment and bias, especially in rural areas. Of course, as an anxious mother I read "harassment" and think "violence" might be a better word.

Most transgender people come out to their family and friends but not their employer or coworkers.

And back and forth it goes. The discussion reminds me of the way the media talks about exercise—do short, intense workouts; no, take lots of short walks all day at a moderate pace; work out an hour each day; no, just thirty minutes three days a week is fine.

The answer must be arrived at on an individual basis.

For additional guidance I began exploring disclosure rules in a range of professions: When should a lawyer reveal that he knows his client has done something awful or tell a judge that he has a conflict of interest in a case? How about a psychiatrist who feels her client might turn violent? And, of course, the medical profession must weigh huge questions when it comes to whether or not to tell a cancer patient he has no chance, or a woman that her husband will not make it. When do you disclose these hard truths? *First, do no harm*, as the Hippocratic oath says. But which is more harmful: disclosure or discretion?

One summer while Donald was still in college I went to an island in

New Hampshire with a boyfriend and his two young sons, both under age twelve. We spent a week in a cabin, with about thirty other people on the island with us, each in their own cabins, but we all united at meal time. My boyfriend's sons only knew Donald as my son. I didn't really think about it one way or another; it just happened naturally that way because when they saw Donald, they saw a man.

At one point I was chatting with a group of mothers while watching a camp volleyball game, and it came up that one of them had gone to my high school and we had some mutual friends. Since Donald had also attended my alma mater, Loomis, that also came up.

The woman's entire energy shifted as I stood there chatting idly about Donald. In that moment I knew that she knew our story, that our mutual friend must have talked about the journey Donald and I went on together while he was in high school, the hard times, the tough decisions, the first person in the school's 150-year history to come out as transgender.

Without hesitating, I brought up that Donnie was now in college and really enjoyed his school because it was very LGBTQ friendly and he is transgender. I let it slip in there like a glass of water on a hot summer day, meant to take the edge off, meant as a kind offering. And she took it without hesitation—open, friendly, and apparently relieved that I had chosen disclosure and done so with comfort and confidence.

But at the close of the conversation I felt that I had to tell her not to tell her young sons who played with my boyfriend's kids because they did not know and might find it all very confusing if they did.

I switched from disclosure to discretion in less than a minute.

Donald himself moved from being a young woman with a girlhood to a trans man with no boyhood in the span of about a year. This history further complicates the disclosure/discretion game. When should I reveal that I raised a daughter when I'm circulating with people who see me with a son? To never bring that up feels like a form of shunning, a death for something I loved above all else in my life. People might presume you simply switch the name and pronouns and get on it, but those who would say such glib things have never had to negate a past girlhood for the sake of a current manhood.

When Donald comes home to visit, I must remember to put away the photographs of J., the daughter he used to be. I have many albums stored in a cedar chest of baby pictures; my four-year-old girl in her Halloween costume, my eight-year-old girl playing in a blue boat at the lake, my twelve-year-old girl graduating middle school. But any image of his past life as a girl unsettles him, which, of course means that there is no childhood for Donald as a boy, no reference point for a young Donald versus an adult Donald.

✦ ✦ ✦

We moved from the South to New England when J. was fourteen, leaving behind nearly everyone who had ever known my child as a daughter and girl. The first time I returned to visit, I reflexively answered the question "So how is J.?" with pat replies. *Fine. Navigating a demanding high school. Volunteering at the theater.* In friends' minds, they were still adding to the narrative they knew as J., the golden-red-haired girl with the green eyes whom their daughters played with on the neighborhood trampoline.

But I knew that narrative had come to a full stop, like a period at the end of an incomplete sentence.

With each subsequent visit I started shutting down the narrative known as J. and building a new storyline known as Donald, my trans son. The people who cared about us did not get in the way of this shift, though the physical distance and this sudden, new timeline for a young man who was once a girl made it harder for most friends to follow along. Donald and I lost touch with almost all of them. When I visit the area now, even I sometimes have trouble believing that I ever lived the life of a mom with a daughter who used to play broomball in the cul de sac with me after school.

Dealing with the issue of J.'s transition should be easier when it comes to strangers who have no inkling of our past and present, but it is not, because for most of us there are only two gender categories. When my last book, *American Idle: A Journey Through Our Sedentary Culture*, came out, I traveled the country as a guest speaker for two years and invariably people would ask, "Do you have any children?" Yes, one, I'd say. "A boy or a girl?"

Think of all that is inferred by that simple question: You have a boy or a girl in diapers. You have a boy or a girl learning to walk. You have a boy or a girl who just braved his or her first day of school. You have a boy or a girl who plays on a sports team, loves an instrument, or embraces the theater.

You have a boy or a girl.

Sometimes I deflect the question, not out of shame or shyness, but simply because the situation doesn't call for any depth or true connection. I might say, "My Donnie is in college now," or something like that so I never directly say if I have a son or daughter. On occasion someone does retort, "So he's in school," with an emphasis on the pronoun.

More recently I have noticed that I give different answers depending on the time period the stranger asks about.

Yes, we used to summer at a lake in New Hampshire before my divorce, and J. loved to play on the rope swing or canoe with a friend to pick blueberries on the island.

Yes, J. deeply disliked the mind games girls played in middle school and stayed off online social sites like Facebook without being asked. She figured she'd be bullied and mocked.

Yes, J. has a childhood I can give you in story form.

Yes, Donnie is in college now and loves the city.

Yes, Donnie works so hard to help with the cost of college.

Yes, Donnie is funny, a fine student, has plenty of friends. He joined a fraternity that he loves.

Yes, a fraternity. In this new narrative line, J.'s story has ended and Donald's past has begun.

At the New Hampshire vacation camp, I brought up the fact that I have a trans son with a stranger because we had a mutual friend who knew our story, but I almost never do that. Peculiar things happen to people's body language when I move this directly to the truth. Most of the real feelings come through the face, the confusion in the eyes, the earnest effort not to react or seem judgmental or surprised. They really do not want to miss a beat and come across as transphobic. But I know I have made them uncomfortable, and many do not even truly know how they feel about such a turn of events in the conversation, in our society.

One of the most complex social groups I deal with is the distant relations I might hear from every two or three years, like a cousin in San Diego or New Haven. They send the Christmas Letter. They ask about J. They know she's getting older and must "be out of college now!" Sometimes they even call because they'll be in town. How's the family? Your mom? Your siblings? Your daughter?

I feel like shouting, "We've crossed into a different Gender Zone!" All of your saved Christmas letters from us tell you that I had a daughter, but that past is wrong. I was raising a trans child all along but just didn't know it.

These distant family relations hear the story, try to catch up, but slip up again and again. They still ask after J. They sometimes correct themselves, but it's all too hard to pin down, to give away a daughter's childhood and replace it with a trans man's present. Some manage to shift to the correct name but almost never to the correct pronoun.

My immediate family has fully embraced the transition story now after many rough years when some of us thought J. was moving too fast to become Donald and was too young to make such radical changes to her/his body. Some of us thought it was a passing phase; some accepted it immediately, in part because they weren't all that emotionally invested in J. to begin with, so they didn't feel they were losing anything.

My ninety-year-old mother wept when she heard that her beloved granddaughter wanted to be embraced as a grandson. For many months, my mom went through a strange period of grief, continuing to reach out and embrace J. as Donald but mourning the slipping away of all evidence of J. as a girl. The golden-red hair became a cropped buzz cut and the gift of a Vera Bradley bag got stowed in the closet.

It was as though in a matter of days she had held a funeral for one grandchild and then crafted a new memory book for a different grandchild. I was astounded at how smoothly she pulled this off, the eldest of the extended family, the one with the longest track record of loss (two husbands, most of her friends, several of her siblings) on a racetrack to a new space so she wouldn't lose her grandchild entirely.

My ninety-year-old mother was the first to bring Donald to buy clothes in the men's department.

My ninety-year-old mother was the first to tell me to my face without flinching that J. was never coming back and Donald was here to stay and I must accept it.

My ninety-year-old mother still talks about when J. was a child and visited her in Florida or lost to her at Scrabble or went to New York City to watch the Christmas show at Radio City Music Hall and bought a ten-dollar chocolate-covered strawberry at Rockefeller Center. One strawberry for ten dollars! They photographed it before eating it.

She shifts more easily than I do between such recollections of her beloved granddaughter's past and the reality of now. She has a wry quality about her whenever she talks about any of it, as though after nine decades it's not that she's seen everything, but that she has somehow weathered all that she has seen.

Just last year she disclosed to me that one of her sisters also has a transgender grandchild; my aunt's son's son became a woman named M.

I know that someplace in the future people will be more accepting of this entire process, the shifting gender continuum, and won't flinch when asked to overlook the fact that the man in front of them had a girlhood not a boyhood. But in these years of transition, and our growing but limited awareness about transgender people, in this window where my daughter, J., is still someone that many people knew even just a handful of years ago, I must move like water myself, flowing in this direction and that depending on the shape of the moment.

Among various professions, when it comes to disclosure, safety and context are everything, but even those measures change radically, especially when you look at how transgender people are treated globally. Even the most basic online search brings up color-coded charts and maps of the world that make it clear that most of Africa, India, and the Middle East consider sexual relations between two people of the same sex illegal. If I shift my focus to something more relevant to our family situation—gender expression—things muddy quickly.

Some countries that might put a person in prison for having homosexual relations, actually accept a person's right to change gender. But—and this is where I must step back and catch my breath—some of these same countries require people to have themselves sterilized before the government will acknowledge their new gender.

Require.

I felt marginalized when teachers, advisors, and counselors kept me out of the conversation about Donald's transition because he was sixteen, and they had no legal right to disclose anything to me, his mother. But at least I knew he was *choosing* his way to his new identity.

In such environments, a misstep along the line between disclosure and discretion could result in a person losing complete control over his or her own body. In India, for example, authorities would have *made* him shut down his ovaries.

Of course the US State Department and local registries of motor vehicles want full disclosure for official documents, such as a passport or driver's license, but the system hasn't caught up with Donald's reality. He's changed his name and presents as male, but he had to go through an incredible series of steps to finally shift from female-to-male on his driver's license. I know he'd probably be offended to know that I feel the state should take care with such things. Not that I would wish the state to deny an individual such rights to choose and shift, but I still feel some deliberation makes sense, especially for people under age twenty-five.

I must also acknowledge that trying to get a new gender designation all lined up on everything—Social Security, driver's license, passport—created bureaucratic inconsistencies in Donald's record that have made him a target for skittish public officials in our post-9/11 world.

Are you a man or a woman?

Somehow the answer to that question doesn't seem a matter of national security, and Donald feels targeted, feels sneaky, feels uncomfortable. When he has the choice, he opts for the bus.

To remind myself how prejudiced and off such inquiries must feel to Donald, I consider that if he were a lesbian, there would be no disconnect on his official identification, no new information to "disclose." Society and official agencies really do need to catch up. Perhaps Facebook's fifty-plus categories for gender aren't as farfetched as they feel to me. Perhaps agencies should just ask for gender identity, as many college applications do now, and let the person fill in what fits, or drop the question of gender entirely.

✦   ✦   ✦

I almost didn't write these essays, which disclose so much about what Donald and I think about what happened to our family as he went through his transition. I thought we could work it out, that we were that close. But the breaks between us started to feel permanent. The decision to use something we both love—writing—to truly divulge the full measure of our feelings engendered more compassion and empathy between us.

But is this more public conversation the right way to go? I felt cynical, even angry, when, in 2015, I heard that Bruce Jenner planned to talk about being transgender with Diane Sawyer on national television. *Right*, I thought, *he's eager for fame, money, and as much attention as possible.* I judged his decision to disclose with a ruthlessness that surprised me.

Then I watched the interview in May of that year, along with nearly a hundred million other people, and his sincerity came through. When Sawyer asked Jenner if he were a reporter what question he would have asked, he replied, "Are you going to be okay?" So Sawyer asked the question and, after a pregnant pause, Jenner answered it.

"I hope so," he said. "I feel like I'm going to be okay."

I felt teary-eyed with empathy.

But I was also struck by the interview with Jenner's former wife, Kris, which popped up on social media a few days after his interview. She wept while one of her daughters from the famous Kardashian clan reprimanded her for not accepting the situation.

So it's okay to disclose you're transgender, I thought as I watched, *but not okay for family members to disclose their grief over the person and relationship they've lost?* I've experienced the same sort of reprimanding looks and comments whenever I openly mourn the loss of my J.

Sometimes when we celebrate openness for a marginalized group, we wind up marginalizing someone else. The conversation around all of this continues to lack nuance and sophistication.

We all circulate within several social circles—family, friends, neighbors, coworkers—and when it comes to transgender rights, each circle can have conflicting social ground rules.

- Christian bakery owners don't want to be forced to craft wedding cakes for gay or transgender couples.
- The US Supreme Court rules that same-sex marriage is now legal in all fifty states.
- Employers in many states can still discriminate against transgender workers and refuse them employment.
- President Obama signed a law making it illegal to discriminate against transgender people employed by the federal government.
- Landlords in many states can refuse to lease to LGBTQ applicants.
- When Donald flies back to LA after visiting me at home, he can legally use a men's restroom in a Connecticut airport but not in North or South Carolina when he stops to catch a connecting flight.

I use bullets to capture the tennis ball–like bounce to all of this. One reason for the disconnect: We have few positive avenues for honest conversation. Everyone digs in with hard-and-fast points of view and shows little respect for the other side. We demonize each other.

Like some right-wing baker in Georgia, I deeply disagreed with my daughter's decision to change her name. I wept over the fact she would no long have my father's initials—JFC—and took on a name I had never even heard mentioned in our home. Now I see that the name was one of the first tools she had at her disposal to act on her need to alter her identity. I can still feel my sadness, the regret, but I dropped the judgment.

But I started with a value system handed down to me from generations of my family. My shift took time. I gave myself permission to work through my own transition in values and found it only here, in these essays, certainly not from the professional medical world. I entered into a conversation with myself because I could not find space to safely enter into that conversation anywhere else, except among some very close friends and family.

I still wrestle with the question, when does discretion tip into deceit? I had a mixed-race student who came to class for months with blue eyes and then suddenly came to class with brown. In an essay for the course she confessed that she idolized the white Barbie-doll ideal and had worn tinted contacts to make herself feel prettier.

We all hide things—hair color, eye color. Now we can add gender to the list.

The freer I feel about disclosing that I have a transgender son, no matter the social situation I'm in, the more discretion I show about flashing some of my darker feelings about the entire experience. Some of my closest friends and family were quick to start referring to Donald as my son when in conversation with me. I know they wanted to embrace me, him, and all of our changes without judgment, but the first few times that happened, I felt violated.

How dare you assume that I think I have a son, I thought, an irrational flash of rage that I later realized was really grief over the complete erasure of J.

How could I ever say I have a son when I never had a boy? It simply felt like a smoke-and-mirrors game. Each exchange demanded that I let go of a daughter I knew I had, a sacrifice I could not put into words.

Now I can say with confidence that I have a son, but I also tell people about my daughter's childhood whenever the conversation demands. My revised world view now includes a new gender continuum that can hold these two things in my mind at once. A grown man can have a girlhood.

As a transgender man, Donald has a right to actualize his own identity. As a mother, I also have a right to remember and cherish my baby girl. Those two lines can fit into the same paragraph and not destroy each other.

Rights

✦ ✦ ✦

The phrase *gender confirming* describes any medical process that helps people feel more comfortable with their gender.

Hormone replacement treatment or *therapy (HRT)*, as it relates to trans health care, is a gender-confirming medical process wherein one takes a monitored hormone dose to bring about secondary sex characteristics that align with one's gender identity. *Testosterone* is stereotypically associated with trans men, and *estrogen* with trans women. A more in-depth description of HRT is given further in this section.

HRT is monitored by an *endocrinologist* or "endo," a doctor specially trained to treat *glands*, the organs in our bodies that create hormones. Examples of glands include ovaries, testes, and the pancreas.

Top surgery is a colloquial phrase that refers to any gender-confirming surgery designed to alter the chest. Top surgery can indicate a *double mastectomy*, which removes breast tissue and creates a flat chest, or *breast implants* or *augmentations*.

Right(s)

Mary Collins

An advisor at my daughter J.'s high school dropped me an e-mail about someone named Donnie Collins's college application file. You have the wrong family, I said in a voice mail. I don't know anyone by that name. She never responded. Instead, her boss called me.

Thus began my saga down the wormhole of shifting parental rights for those with children ages sixteen to eighteen. Against my wishes, my daughter had asked her teachers to refer to her by a male name, Donald, and by male pronouns. She also asked the college admissions advising office to allow her to apply to college under her new assumed name.

When J. told me she was transgender, I had never heard of that word and did not grasp what that might entail. We discussed the name change, but I begged to have J. slow down, to wait until starting college to pull the switch, when it would be a natural new starting point. I thought she/he had agreed.

Then, the phone call.

It turns out that at school she had been a he for months, but no one had told me because under Connecticut law, a high school does not have to share such things with a parent if the student is sixteen or older. Donald did have to wait until age eighteen to make the legal name change on his own, but by his junior year, he had the right to be called by whatever name or pronoun he chose at school.

The fact that he was at a boarding school and never attended public schools in Connecticut meant I also never got to know any other parents, who might have heard about what was going on and made some effort to communicate with me.

It proved a perfect storm for an information whiteout.

I had hoped Donald would use a name more like his legal name, something he said he would consider. But he wound up using new first and middle names that I had never heard him mention. Only now, years later, do I see what an impossible half-step I was asking him to take, the word "trans" on my tongue for the first time, my biggest concern still to protect J., not to help craft Donald.

Two years later, in front of a judge in my hometown in the state where four previous generations of my father's family had resided, without me there or without my consent, my high-school-aged daughter took her next bold step toward becoming a man and legally changed her name to Donald Oliver Collins. The irony: He inadvertently cut off the only connection we had to a positive male role model in our lives, my beloved father, who had died when I was fourteen. He and J. had shared the same initials and the same middle name, something Donald discarded.

✦ ✦ ✦

The backstory for the biological father is complicated, a tale of an old friend whom I hadn't seen in a decade coming back into my life for what proved to be a life-altering month fling. I got pregnant using birth control. We agreed to keep the baby, but I knew I did not love this man and made it clear from the moment we saw the positive test that I would not marry him. Life with a gun-toting, dog-loving, truck-driving guy wouldn't have been good for me, and my unhappiness would not have been good for him. After six months of jostling back and forth on what to do about the baby, he walked away.

No wedding meant no help and, as it turns out, no involvement with J. whatsoever, even though I pleaded with him to stay in his own child's life.

It turns out that biological dads have few responsibilities if they do not marry the mother, whereas, under American and international law, the mother must step up and accept full responsibility for housing, feeding, clothing, and educating her child. I considered the father a good friend, and I wanted him to stay involved. But when he left, without any offer of child support, I let him go, full of guilt over my lack of commitment to building a family with him. I regret only the guilt because, I felt, he had a responsibility to his biological child no matter what happened between the two of us.

It took generations of women to earn me the right to refuse to marry or live with the biological father of my child; many countries today would not even grant me that freedom. Only now, reflecting on all that Donald did to win his new name, despite our close relationship and all that I have done for my child, do I see a parallel between our decisions. In each instance, we respected and valued the other person— in my case, the father of J.; in Donald's case, me—but acted to realize some basic right in our own lives. The father never saw this, and I did not see it when Donald so aggressively severed my parental control over his life.

My child's biological father loved me, and I loved my child, but love bestows no rights. The father thought because I valued and admired him as a friend and bore his child, that I had to stay. I thought that because the most emotionally tender moments of my life came while reading to my young daughter, that she would always be with me, and by *with me* I mean emotionally, physically, morally, and intellectually. When J. did something so fundamental to her identity without me, it shook me to the core, and I have never recovered.

Whenever I tried to speak with other adults outside my extended family about my experiences raising my trans son, people invariably would chime, "Oh, she'll outgrow it," or, "Kids go to such lengths for attention," or, "It's a phase." But I had more respect for my child's seriousness and self-awareness than that and knew it was never going to stop at the name change.

And it didn't.

For all of human history, across most cultures and religions, parents' rights over their young children have been sacrosanct. A cursory comparison of the Bible and Qur'an, for example, show tremendous overlap. In Islam, one story recounts how a man asks the prophet whom should he show the most kindness and the prophet responds, "Your mother." The man asks the question again, and the prophet says, "Your mother." And again. "Your mother." Only on the fourth inquiry does the prophet say, "Your father."

And, of course, in Christianity, to honor thy father and mother is the Fifth Commandment from God. And why? "So that your days may be long upon the land which the Lord your God is giving you."

The second part of that commandment infers that you're not long for this world if you are disrespectful toward your parents, probably more of a reality in the much more violent ancient world, where kin and tribes ruled. Now we live in a world of nations governed by laws, which in some instances can override the authority of parents.

Obviously, many of these laws are in place to protect children from abusive relatives. To my shock, I learned in online conversations that many people assume that transgender men who go through all the aggressive changes that Donald has gone through, including steroid shots, a double mastectomy, and a hysterectomy, must come from abusive households. Once a woman even told me that to my face when she heard I had a transgender son.

"All the people I know that are like that were sexually abused as kids," she said.

The world of law over the world of tribal and parental rights saves abused children, who can become wards of the state. I have heard plenty of stories of overly controlling, vicious parents who are shocked when their son or daughter turns sixteen or eighteen and takes advantage of his or her newfound rights to do everything possible to snub, hurt, disrespect, and disown the mother and/or father. I firmly believe that J. was not doing anything remotely like that. At the time that's how it felt, but now, with more distance from all that happened, I believe our parallel acts of independence—me setting off on my own as a single parent, J./Donald setting off on an identity quest that he grasped but I did not understand—have more in common with each other than I like to admit. I did not act to hurt the father; I acted to protect my own life and happiness. Donald did not act to hurt me; he acted to find his authentic self.

But knowing this does not stop me from becoming defensive about the sentiment that Donald was a victim of abuse. I feel obliged to make my case that J. and then Donald received the full measure of my attention and devotion, despite having started out as a single-parent household with no child support.

The first step I took was to walk away from a writing career that had begun gaining momentum after my first book. I moved from Washington, DC, to New England to live with one of my sisters so I could be at home with my baby full time. I turned down some amazing jobs, including one at Harvard, to honor my responsibilities as sole caretaker. I did this willingly and by choice, grateful to somehow work out a way to spend as much time as possible with my child.

My mother embraced her charming grandchild as firmly as any grandparent could. My siblings cared about their roles as extended family and brought J. on trips and tried to bridge the age gap between the cousins (my daughter was the youngest) by including J. on many family adventures.

Of course the biological father had walked, a level of rejection I cannot imagine since my own father offered only unconditional love. There was no male figure for J. to give her candy or meet her after school. Later, when a stepfather came into the picture, then wound up several states away after a divorce, it was another leave-taking, another incomplete emotional connection.

But our dad deficit was no greater than many other weighty things children in the world must bear. On a day-to-day basis, J. had a stable home, spent the bulk of her childhood in the same town, and had a biological parent fully engaged in her welfare.

To presume abuse presumes mental illness and great dysfunction, but I know Donald discounts this theory and sees himself as being the product of a normal household. In his view, no amount of counseling can get at his "problem" because being transgender is not a problem.

And for those who presume that my child must have sprung from a brutal home environment, I can only say that I have never loved anything more in my life than my only child and I gave her all I had to offer emotionally and financially.

I took J.'s right to an education so seriously that when a second-grade teacher told me to get my intelligent, creative, super-sensitive child out of the public schools, I did. It took a team of people to pull off a first-rate education for J. and, later, Donald, but in my darkest moments, when I felt completely marginalized as a parent, I took great solace in the fact I was doing all I could to give him a tremendous education.

Another primary responsibility as Donald's sole parent, good health care, proved the most vexing.

What's good health care when a clinic will give your eighteen-year-old child male hormones with few questions asked just six weeks after he's first arrived to college in a big city?

What's good health care when a doctor is willing to strip your child's body of perfectly sound parts so his physical self can better match his gender identity?

Once Donald turned eighteen, none of those doctors ever had an obligation to consult me on anything or answer anything I might ask. More germane to this essay is that when Donald was sixteen, a counselor sent him to an LGBTQ support group led by people who had transitioned from one sex to another and celebrated anyone else in the group with the courage to do the same. I know some of those people are heroes to Donald, but to me they took over my parental rights at the very moment I should have been able to exercise them most vigorously. Since I did not agree with the groupthink, I felt ostracized. Parents who embraced all of it gave me the silent treatment.

There has to be a middle ground.

At age twenty-two, when Donald was firmly his own person legally and emotionally, he elected to have a hysterectomy. I could not bring myself to assist in the sterilization of my only child, so I did not drive him to the procedure or pick him up afterward. I marked the occasion in my own way: by burning a baby picture of my lovely daughter down to ash, then spreading the ashes around a favored rose bush in my yard. I did it at night, the flames licking the side of a stainless steel pan that I often used to cook pasta. In that moment, I also showed caring and love as I honored the daughter in Donald and my child's ability to bear children.

All turned to ash.

Donald went out of his way to show me great respect through his other actions. He worked hard as a scholarship student, spent two years as a resident assistant in his dorm, a grueling way to earn room and board. He never became aggressive, angry, or rude when I disagreed with his decision to have the surgeries.

Yet, he stripped me of my rights as a parent to achieve his goal and used others to help him do it. At the time, I thought it was the worst thing that anyone could have ever done to me. But what would Donald's biological father say to me, the mother of his child, who refused to marry him? Did he feel stripped of all of his dignity by my rejection, and by most of his rights, a move so demoralizing that he never sought to reclaim any of them, even though I welcomed his involvement in our child's day-to-day care and lived within miles of him for twelve of our daughter's first fourteen years of life?

Our hard-won rights to be transgender, to be a single mother, to be so many special things in American society come with great costs. Part of me finds myself looking up parents' rights advocacy groups online, wondering how my child becoming sixteen could result in such a draconian flip, in which in one month I am fully in control and ever mindful of her best interests, and in another so marginalized that I don't even know my own child's name anymore. Based on my cursory research, I realized that most of the parents' rights advocates simply want to homeschool their children (considered legal in the United States since a 1925 Supreme Court ruling) and philosophically sit on the far right of the political spectrum with the anti-choice folks, creationists, and the pro-gun lobby.

That's not a bench I want to sit on.

But the marginalization I have experienced further motivates me to demand a longer bench, a place where someone like me can plead

that the professionals and parents who excised me out of the conversation about my own sixteen-year-old's actions take a harder look at what
they did and what they could have done better to help Donald and me
find common ground. The more they stonewalled me, the more silence
they directed my way, the more I wanted out. Completely. They took
the thing I loved the most in the world away from me without so much
as a phone call. That may have been their legal right and Donald's legal
right, but it's not right.

The conundrum of meeting everyone's rights becomes even more
apparent to me as I reflect on the United Nations' Universal Declaration of Human Rights, first championed and passed under the leadership of Eleanor Roosevelt, herself a great gender bender. A paraphrased
sampler from the thirty rights (in my language and with my thoughts
about them):

2. Don't Discriminate

Twenty years ago—or even more recently than that—Donald would
have faced tremendous discrimination when in high school and college
he transitioned from female to male. In fact, he received resounding
support at each level. I hope the larger society can continue to embrace
our transgender citizens. Even just ten years ago, if I had questioned
what was going on, educators, counselors, and medical professionals
would have rushed to include me, but today they discriminated against
me because I was not fully on board about J.'s transition to Donald
from day one. One gain, one loss.

11. Always Innocent Until Proven Guilty

A complete stranger accused me of raising a child in an abusive household.

Complete strangers accused me of being homophobic and prejudiced whenever I questioned what Donald was doing, especially the
pace at which he moved at such a young age. I am none of those things.

19. Freedom of Expression

My right to engage in this essay project is the most affirming experience I've had as a parent and a human being concerned about the welfare of my child since Donald was fourteen years old. I invited my transgender son to join me with his own words so he, too, could feel freed by honest expression.

30. No One Can Take Your Rights Away

When Donald became eighteen, all my rights as a parent were taken away. That happens for all parents in America, but should it?

To cope, I had to forget about my sense of entitlement as a parent because I loved my child, and, unlike Donald's father, I had decided instead to focus on my duty. This much steadier, deep-seated emotion sustained me during the murkiest moments and most unforgiving hours. I had a responsibility to raise my child to the best of my ability no matter how unexpected the situation, and that basic tenet guided my decision to continue to pay for Donald's education and to continue to try to create a space in my house so we could both still call it home.

On one occasion I crossed paths with a parent who had taken Donald in while he and I were wrestling over the rate of his transition from female to male. For several weeks during his sophomore year in college, I so strongly opposed his decision to inject himself with hormones and surgically alter his body at such a young age that I would not let him come home. I felt as though he wanted me to support something akin to a drug addiction under my own roof.

We both now have a more nuanced understanding of what happened to us and what continues to happen to us, but at the time we had to reach this nadir in our relationship before we could climb to a more affirming, mutually respectful middle ground. My mother—Donnie's Gran—in particular kept hammering home to me that J. and Donald were the same person, and kept reminding Donald that I was grieving the loss of J. and that he must show me more compassion.

A year after this period, I found myself helping Donald move into his dorm room at college. As I waited in the suite's living room, the mother of one of his roommates swung onto a stool next to me, not quite sure who I was.

I introduced myself.

"Oh, you're Donnie's mother," she said, her body rigid with disgust, her voice low and sour.

In her eyes, I had abandoned Donald. She never once thought for a moment that perhaps I was giving all I had, down to my last breath, to save J., my daughter whom she had never known.

"Yes," I replied, my own voice like a fist. "Be careful what you say, because you do not know the whole story."

She walked away.

I continued helping Donald move into his room.

Hidden Fees

Donald Collins

> I've heard parents say all they want is "the best" for their children,
> but the best is subjective and anchored by how they know and
> learned the world.
>
> —Janet Mock, *Redefining Realness*

Spring 2011

The first openly trans adult I ever met was Tony Ferraiolo, a genial trans man in his late forties who co-ran, and still runs, a youth support group for gender-variant teens in the New Haven area. I attended this group on and off my senior year of high school. We all just called it "Group."

Originally, Tony told me, Group started with him and two members but grew within a year to encompass dozens of participants of all identities and backgrounds. He even started a group for parents and an art-based one for younger kids.

When I found out about Group and told my mom I wanted to go, she was highly conflicted, but eventually agreed to drive me to the next Saturday meeting. The first time we made the forty-five-minute commute, we got terribly lost and both ended up red-faced and stressed out of our minds. It reminded me of a game I played when I was younger, where I would leave the radio on an annoying station and see how long before my mom couldn't take it anymore. It was always a big joke to me, because eventually she would cave and turn the dial.

But on the way to Group, I was terrified she would just say "fuck it" and turn the car around. And it wasn't because of some static-infused banjo riff on FM. We were sitting with my gender trouble, seeing how long we could both last before something had to give.

"I don't know if I'm the best parent in the world or the worst," she sighed as we parked across the street from the meeting location.

I didn't think she was either; I just wanted to get the heck out of the car.

Down the block I saw Tony outside the meeting address, stocky, bearded, and tattooed, emanating this energetic warmth. I remember thinking, to quote Liz Lemon, "I want to go to there."

I only attended Group for a couple of months, but knew the formula well. We went around and introduced ourselves with our name and pronouns, maybe a line about what we liked or where we were from. We shared highs and lows from our week, got words of encouragement from other members and the adult facilitators. Sometimes people cried, really cried, but the mood wasn't always low. Group members mingled afterwards with a kind of ease that you can't cultivate anywhere but a safe space.

✦ ✦ ✦

My mom worried that attending Group would give me ideas and push me headlong into radical decisions. I understood her worry as having two distinct parts:

1. The fear that I was delusional and that Tony and the kids would irresponsibly validate and encourage this delusion to permanent ends.
2. The bigger, more abstract fear that I needed something she couldn't give and that I would seek it out wherever I could find it, whether she was included or not.

✦ ✦ ✦

I have to admit: she was right about that second one.

✦ ✦ ✦

I came out at seventeen. Tony came out later in life, in his early forties, and I always wondered if listening to a bunch of young adults talk about their gender dysphoria was frustrating for him. He never showed anything but patience and care with us. The frustration was my own projection, I think, as I personally always wished I had come out sooner and avoided the hell on earth of my first puberty. I held a kind of oscillating envy towards kids in the group who were younger and more "ahead" than me, or whose parents had pledged acceptance and advocacy off the bat. The over-comparative tendencies of those years was (and maybe still is?) pretty normal but ultimately unproductive.

Rather than urging me down new, corrupting paths, Group gave me company on the path I was on. I met other kids who shared aspects of my identity, who needed the same things I did. Even better, I met trans kids whose identities were entirely different than mine and who needed completely different things for themselves. In a journey that began at Group, and continues still, I learned that "trans" didn't mean the same thing to everyone.

At the time, as much as I loved the queer space, I didn't want to *be* queer. I wanted to be the Most Regular Boy in the World. If these kids wanted to live queer, I thought, more power to them. But I would be *better*; I would blend and blend until I had nothing in common with them anymore. I was filled with anger and frustration directed at my body and its refusal to command the male social validation I needed. I may have identified as trans, but I was far from understanding that identity in context. I was a hypocrite, steeped in toxic stereotypical ideas about gender, and my discomfort with queerness stemmed from this combination of pain and lack of education. You can't value a space outside yourself and devalue that same space within yourself.

✦ ✦ ✦

The summer of 2011, I left the circle of Group, my immediate family, and all their disconnections for my college (and gender) future in Boston. Throughout the next four years, I incurred many costs—financial, emotional, and physical. Sometimes I wondered if I could pay them all, and if it was even worth it. I'm still paying, and it's still worth it.

Puzzling my way through medical institutions and private practices, reaching out blindly to LGBTQ orgs, untangling the red tape, and making it all work, I acutely noticed the absence of my mom. Yet I was never alone, and during my transition I built some of the strongest friendships of my life. These friendships, including those at Group, often became their own sources of conflict. My mother felt cast aside and disrespected when other families provided the support and encouragement she could not.

Writing this book and looking back on the milestones of my transition, I'm not judging my words and actions but instead interrogating their meanings. My favorite professor, Tulasi Srinivas, uses the word "parse" to this effect: *to examine or analyze minutely.* It is this analysis, constantly evolving, inherently self-absorbed and self-bettering, that has led me to a contextual understanding of my own identity and of the barriers my mother and I faced as I claimed it.

12/2/2011

To get pumped up before my first endocrinology appointment, I gave myself a haircut.

I had been long possessed by the notion that if I could just get my hair short enough, that if my short hair looked *just right*, people would understand that I was a boy, and all the confusion would be over. This never happened, and my shoddy, uneven haircuts made me even more self-conscious, projecting the barely-getting-out-of-bed aesthetic only severe depression can cultivate.

My hair has always been something of a miniature battleground between my mother and me. As a child, I expressed the desire to cut it more than once, and my dad, Andrew, who raised me in my biological father's absence, would shrug *why not*, but my mom always fought me. The resulting compromise was a *Charlie and the Chocolate Factory* trim, hanging just beneath my ears. It gifted eight-year-old me with an androgynous surfer vibe and contributed to an (admittedly) outstanding second-grade class photo of me in a Hawaiian shirt.

I ended up covering my homespun buzz cut with a brandless,

baby-blue snapback in keeping with my "it's a boy!" look for the trip, along with baby-blue checked shirt, baby-blue sweater. I don't even look good in the color.

In preparation for the endocrinology appointment, I had saved up my class skips. I left early the day before, catching a bus to New Haven, where my friend Skylar's family picked me up. The plan was to stay the night with them and make the short drive to the doctor in the morning before catching a bus back to Boston.

✦ ✦ ✦

I met Skylar Spear on my first day at Group, and he became one of my closest friends. When we met, he was a handsome fifteen-year-old with great socks and a prodigious LGBTQ advocacy record. Neither of us had started hormones, although we both wanted to. Over the next several years, he became my best friend, my benchmark, and my sibling.

During the Group stage of our friendship, I struggled with comparisons. I admired Skylar greatly and wanted to be more like him. He "passed" better than me, and his family was bigger than mine and supportive of his gender. He seemed to have a grip on himself when I was still in a place of shame and confusion. He readily accepted the word "queer" as an identifier and was unapologetic about his queerness. And he was three years younger.

Sometimes I had trouble being friends with Skylar and would retreat because I was jealous or sad or too darn concerned with my own problems to recognize that he had his own. Despite my various shortcomings, he treated me with unconditional support and respect, and his family welcomed me at their table.

✦ ✦ ✦

Being trans, I've always, sometimes stubbornly, oriented myself as "behind" in a way. I've had to work extra hard to achieve the things other boys were guaranteed at birth, whether it was body parts, chemistry, a name, or the right to wear baby blue. In college I got pissed when my guy friends, with minimal effort, had the slim, tapered torso I wanted, while I stayed late at the gym. Sometimes I got so caught up in this Me vs. Him vortex that I couldn't celebrate any of my accomplishments. I held my own body and masculinity to a ridiculous standard that I didn't hold anyone else to. I never let myself rest or feel proud, and I burned out because of it.

We're obsessed with the physicality of trans bodies, but so much of the long-haul gender-identity work is mental and emotional.

✦ ✦ ✦

At the time of my endocrinology appointment, my mother and I weren't doing great. I had begun my freshman year at Emerson College in the Visual Media Arts program, where I was pursuing a BA in screenwriting. I lived in the largest dorm on campus, ironically called the Little Building.

"I know what you're thinking, but it's named after a man and not its size," I would later recite on campus tours.

In the LB, I occupied a single room on the seventh floor, which was weird. Most freshmen live in doubles, triples, or suites. But since my gender hadn't been legally changed, the college told me they couldn't allow me to room with boys; freshman rooming was same-gender only. It was girls or a single. I love girls, but after four years in high school women's dormitories, I picked the single.

Even at a "progressive" and LGBTQ-friendly college like Emerson, these restrictive policies exist. They lurk in the back files of higher administration until some queer kid trips the wire.

✦ ✦ ✦

My mom moved me in, and we corresponded during my first few weeks at Emerson. In November, my birthday month, I called to tell her I was starting testosterone. I had scheduled an appointment with a well-known doctor in the New Haven area, recommended to me by some people from Group.

I don't think she was surprised. We had discussed early on her opinion that I should "wait" until graduating college before making any alterations to my body. Four years without progress on my terms meant four years wasted. Four unhappy years. I couldn't handle it.

My mom emotionally reiterated her opinion regarding physical changes, this time with a new action stage: *She* didn't feel comfortable having me in her home if I was starting hormones. *She* couldn't handle it. But, as she pointed out, I was legally eighteen.

"You can do what you want," she said sadly, a statement rather than the endorsement I wanted.

The call marked the beginning of a six-month period of estrangement. We didn't talk to or see each other. I didn't go home for my birthday and spent Christmas and New Year's at a friend's house. The Spearses and my endocrinologist were only forty minutes from my mom's, but I didn't consider reaching out to her when my bus arrived in New Haven.

Time and again, during our mending years, I felt the burden of tearing open the wound by bringing my medical experiences into the room. Things are good: "Mom, I'm getting top surgery." Things are good: "Mom, I'm having a hysterectomy."

Family members encouraged me to stay strong regarding my relationship with my mom, and I know they said the same to her. My grandmother and aunt were instrumental in helping maintain the delicate balance, emphatically supporting us both as we tried to work it out. But I never got the feeling my family wanted to hear about the ins and outs of my trans life; rather, I got the explicit sense that they *didn't*.

It seemed natural then that I would gravitate towards Skylar and his family. Theirs was a living room where queer stuff was just a part of the conversation, not a conversation stopper. I could express myself and inhabit my cherished normality at the same time.

✦   ✦   ✦

The Spears are a rare, dynamite combination of rural and urbane. They live in a pastoral town outside New Haven, where they have a vegetable garden and a massive dog named Ajax. In another life, I can see our two families sharing hikes, dinners, and movie nights. Skylar's mom participates in local politics and runs an agricultural high school. His sister studies zoology, and his stepfather helps companies responsibly manage their toxic waste. Everything in their house is organic or vegan-friendly. They're like human trees, soaking up bad vibes and putting out good ones.

The morning of my endocrinology appointment, they scrambled to iron out logistics. Skylar had school, and his mom, Melissa, and step-dad, Roger, were taking their own cars to work.

"Why don't you take the van?" Melissa suggested, offering up the only other vehicle they had.

"Sure," I said, trying to sound chill.

The van was an empty white Ford, some years old, sitting up off the path of their driveway. I had never driven a van before, only my AAA driving school's long-suffering Mitsubishi Lancer and my mom's Volvo station wagon.

Like most manual cars, the Spears' Ford had idiot-proof gear options. I just so happened to be immune and chose "L," eventually correcting my mistake a few strained miles down the road. I had a car phase in my masculinity spiral, but I think I missed the practical points.

The drive was mercifully short. I found my doctor's address, parked, and waited. I was almost an hour early. Skylar texted me good luck.

✦ ✦ ✦

Dr. H. is like the human embodiment of a cheerful wink. I trusted him immediately, though the stuffy atmosphere of his waiting room didn't forecast his winning character. Small TVs showed close-captioned talk shows and last year's *People* magazines were spread out on tables. Everyone there, except for another trans person my age, looked over sixty and struggling. The woman at reception exhibited saintly patience as I fished out ID cards from my overstuffed backpack.

Dr. H. sat with me for an hour, explaining how testosterone worked, why I was starting at the dose he was prescribing, and when my blood would be tested. He drew a little picture of a line graph, a floating hill representing the effects of T in my system over the two-week shot intervals.

"The goal," he explained, "is that your waves aren't too up and down. We want the shots to keep the level of T in your body as consistent as possible."

Health-care professionals like Dr. H., who are welcoming, communicative, and trans-positive, are in high demand and short supply.

✦ ✦ ✦

Diabetes is the most common endocrine disorder, followed by thyroid diseases like goiter and Hashimoto's. Hormone replacement treatment, as developed for non-trans people, started in the 1930s to aid menopausal women and men with hypergonadism. Around this time, trans medicine was just getting on its feet.

One of the most famous endocrinologists in this new field was Harry Benjamin (1885–1986), a German-born doctor and colleague of Magnus Hirschfeld (1868–1935), the renowned sexologist whose Berlin-based Institute for Sexual Science pioneered the study and understanding of gender and sexual diversity. Nazis burned the institute's library in 1933, which led Hirschfield to flee for France, where he would remain until his death, two years later. Benjamin set up practice in San Francisco, where he soon became known as "the leading medical authority on transsexuality," collaborating with other progressives such as Alfred Kinsey.

However, while Benjamin advanced the medical interest and understanding of trans health needs, he also contributed to a set of treatment guidelines that placed psychiatrists and doctors in total control of who was allowed medical treatment.

Trans people who were "chosen" for surgical and hormonal treatments had to check off a ridiculous list of prerequisites to please their cis gatekeepers. Ambitious physicians and researchers thus exploited a desperate population; those willing to submit to observation and invasive research in order to get medical care.

The *Diagnostic and Statistical Manual of Mental Disorders* (*DSM*) sets the medical-industry standard for diagnosis and treatment "for every psychiatric disorder recognized by the U.S. healthcare system." Until 2012, "gender identity disorder" (GID) was the diagnosis for trans people. When I was approved for my top surgery, my insurance validated me as a "true transsexual," a phrase that goes all the way back to Benjamin's 1966 book *The Transsexual Phenomenon*. The *DSM* has since replaced GID with "gender dysphoria," attempting to acknowledge the emotional distress of gender dissonance and not infer mental illness.

In May 2016 Lambda Legal released an updated (and free) publication called *Creating Equal Access to Quality Health Care for Transgender Patients*, intending to aid physicians and medical centers in effectively and respectfully treating trans patients. The updated release followed on the heels of the Obama administration confirming discrimination protections for LGBTQ people in medical environments under the Affordable Care Act.

The safety of trans people in health care and the controlling way health-care systems treat trans people are coming under scrutiny and are on the slow road to reform. But a diagnosis is absolutely still needed to attain treatment promptly and legally. I've had four therapists, two psychiatrists, three general physicians, three endocrinologists, and two surgeons, and they were always sending each other letters about me.

✦ ✦ ✦

Today, hormone replacement is becoming a more culturally recognized option in trans-related health care; however, in part due to the recentness of its acceptability, we still don't know a lot about its long-term effects. We *do* know, through the use of hormone therapy in cis men and women, as treatment for menopause, prostate cancer, or chronic "low" hormone levels, that there *can* be significant risks, including an increased likelihood for cancer and cardiac problems.

Like the word "trans," hormone treatment is different for everyone and should ideally be tailored to an individual. Not everyone needs it or wants it, and there is a broad range of starting doses. Hormones can be administered by shot, taken orally as a tablet, rubbed on in the form of a gel, and even time-released subdermally via surgically inserted "pellets."

People are often surprised to learn that I will take hormones for the rest of my life. For me, right now, that means a shot a week. Since I've had a hysterectomy, without testosterone, my body would produce no dominant hormone on its own, which is *not healthy* and can lead to osteoporosis (brittle bones). I also really *like* the chronic effects of being on T. Some changes, like my lower voice, are permanent, but others, like my weight and muscle distribution, only occur if I maintain my levels. For trans people on estrogen (E), these effects are different: hair and skin soften, breast tissue develops, muscle mass decreases, and fat moves to the butt and thighs. The voice, however, is unaffected by E, and many trans women arduously modulate and train their voices to a higher, more stereotypically "feminine" range.

As of 2016, I have been on T for five years, firmly monitored by health-care systems. To get this care covered, I have literally run all over for consultations, taken trains and buses to doctors, switched policies, switched back, won some claims, lost others, and sacrificed around 75 percent of my credit on the blue "medical" slice of my bank's pie-graph spending report.

Treatment, and the ability to tailor it safely, is a massive issue of access and privilege in the trans community. According to the National Transgender Discrimination Survey, 20 percent of trans respondents reported being uninsured. Among those incarcerated, 17 percent reported being denied hormones outright. And although 62 percent overall had experienced hormone therapy, respondents weren't asked *how* they got their hormones. Unable to find or fill prescriptions, many trans folks procure through backdoors, sharing with friends, buying online.

✦ ✦ ✦

Testosterone instigated a complete sea change across my entire life. I began to feel invested in my body and actually started taking care of it.

For much of my early transition, I believed in a person no one else could see. I couldn't expect my mother to understand what it feels like to recognize this disconnection in oneself, the disconnection hormone treatment helped me bridge. What I wanted, more than my mom's understanding, was her trust. By not supporting my health-care decisions, I felt my mom didn't trust me to know what was best for myself.

Gradually, over time, my newfound confidence and well-being helped her to reactivate this trust. Though she still does not agree with my surgical decisions, she doesn't deny the significant, positive effect they've had on my quality of life.

7/25/2012

The judge asked for my Social Security number, which I had stored in a note on my phone to keep from forgetting. I read it to him, glancing at the screen.

"You really shouldn't keep that on your phone," the judge chided. "You should have it memorized."

I remember him saying this so clearly, and to this day it still bothers me so much. I've told the interaction to countless people in the hopes that eventually I will crack that mysterious re-memory code, the one that makes dumb tiny things stay with us forever.

Now I'm convinced I remember it because I wanted nothing more in that moment than to say, *Shut the fuck up! Fuck youuu!*

✦ ✦ ✦

The summer of my name change, I worked at a day camp in my hometown of Alexandria, Virginia, with two of my roommates from college. The camp, which I attended as a child, paid well and gave me somewhere to be that wasn't Connecticut. For three months I stayed locally with my dad, Andrew, a native Virginian who champions waterfront conservation and has built shelves especially for his rock collection.

As previously mentioned, my dad is technically my step-dad, as I have never really known my biological father. I met him once at fourteen for Thai food, but it failed to lead to any grand reunion, definitely nothing to make a movie about. My mom didn't want to marry him, and he didn't want a child growing up between two homes, so he stepped back and she had the baby (me!) on her own. We never asked him for any child support, never got any, and when my mom started a conversation about him possibly helping with college, he denied paternity. As a lawyer, he knew the procedures and paperwork required for DNA testing would go past my eighteenth birthday, absolving him of any responsibilities.

"That's pretty douchey," I said when I heard.

"Yeah," my mom had replied on the phone, "it is pretty douchey."

My mother married Andrew when I was five, and they were together on and off for a decade, divorcing when I entered high school. We had some really good years and some bad ones. I never took my parents' divorce personally or too hard, and I don't really consider it a defining point of my adolescence. By the time they separated officially, the wheels had been in motion for a while, and I wasn't stunned. I accept what my mom and Andrew separately contribute to my life and try not to get hung up on some sepia-toned dream of a perfect family (although clearly I struggle sometimes).

Andrew and I correspond long distance, and I see him once or twice a year. We have a good relationship, albeit an incomplete one. He's never been a live-in parent like my mother, whose last name I have and who was always, rightfully, my sole guardian.

That is to say, when I came out as trans to him, the stakes weren't as high.

✦ ✦ ✦

The Alexandria weather was sweltering, sometimes criminally polluted, and I counted my luck to be a computer lab counselor, indoors with air conditioning and access to a ubiquitous amount of cold diet sodas. Somewhat less lucky was the uniform, a jumpsuit orange T-shirt.

If you bind your chest, you come to see single layers as a near impossibility. Beneath my orange staff shirt, I wore an undershirt, two binders, and another undershirt to create the appearance of "nothing."

I frequently slouched, fidgeted, and adjusted when I thought no one was looking. In the heat, I wilted.

My campers tugged at me all summer to swim during the camp's pool period, and I always brushed them off with some excuse.

"I didn't bring my bathing suit," I would say. "I didn't bring a towel."

"You said that six weeks ago," my camper Ryan would counter without fail.

To him, I was just a party pooper.

My torso's miserable quality of life slowly but surely overshadowed my original summer name-change objective. *Imagine this, but with a flat chest*, became the recurring thought. Imagine drinking this coffee *with a flat chest*. Imagine going for that run *with a flat chest*.

My sizable weekly paycheck gave me the confidence to begin planning. It was groundwork only. I could afford my chosen surgeon's hundred-dollar consultation fee and the thousand dollars down to secure a date, but beyond that, I was counting on insurance to come through. And all of it would have to wait until I was back in Massachusetts for my fall semester.

Despite knowing this, I would obsess spasmodically about my surgery planning, tallying payment options on Sticky Notes and napkins, and dumbly berating myself for the merest personal expenses. I didn't need that ice cream; I didn't need that night at the movies. Then I would always return to earth.

My surgery is not going to happen today, tomorrow, or next week.

Yes, I needed to plan, but I also needed to focus on the task at hand. And I was allowed to make the present livable in the meantime.

✦ ✦ ✦

A legal name change required a hearing at my local probate court, which otherwise deals mainly with estates and wills. Since I was a Connecticut resident, that meant taking a train up the coast from Virginia and going to the West Hartford town hall.

To obtain a hearing, I needed to fill out PC-901, the official adult "change of name" form, and send it to the probate court along with my birth certificate and passport. And since I didn't *have* my birth certificate, I contacted Virginia's Office of Vital Records to order another. It cost me a few bucks and, temporarily, my driver's license, which I sent along as identity verification.

My mom kept the original birth certificate at home in my "memory box," and asking her to mail it so I could be Donald on paper was not a phone call I needed to have in my life.

✦ ✦ ✦

As much as I hated having to take a seven-hour train ride to court, I lucked out with my standing as a Connecticut resident.

I've never really considered the state my home but rather like a way station between lives. I didn't grow up there and only moved back to go off to boarding school. Upon arriving from Virginia, I didn't like our drafty colonial house. I never really got to know other kids in town because I spent all my time boarding. These are my spoiled grievances.

In 1992, Connecticut was one of the first states to pass a law explicitly banning discrimination regarding sexual orientation. In 2011, Governor Dannel Malloy signed "An Act Concerning Discrimination," adding gender identity to the list of protections. I remember attending a local ACLU function in celebration and listening to several trans folks speak about their employment experiences, dishing about what corporations to avoid and who had real insurance benefits.

As these people taught me, passing laws didn't guarantee a discrimination-free experience, but it did speak to the state's strong community-based advocacy, and policies worked in tandem with other social-support networks. There are Connecticut chapters of LGBTQ organizations like GLAAD, PFLAG, and GLSEN (Gay, Lesbian and Straight Education Network), as well as information-laden Planned Parenthood chapters and local support groups like the one I attended.

✦ ✦ ✦

One bonus as a Connecticut resident was the state's approachable policy on name changes, which its Supreme Court declared were to be "granted liberally." I imagined an Oprah-like giveaway. Name changes for all. This was optimistic.

The fee to change your name in Connecticut is $225. I gathered together a check, my birth certificate, the completed forms, and my best vibes, sending everything to the probate court. My application was accepted, and I scheduled a hearing a few weeks away, on July 25, got the day off, and booked a train ticket to Hartford. By that point, the process had taken around seven weeks.

As Thomas Page McBee writes in his slow-burning memoir *Man Alive*, "The tasks felt manageable, if endless."

✦ ✦ ✦

On July 25, my friend Helena picked me up early from the train station, all smiles. She and I had met while interning for a local theater my last summer of high school. She was a few years older, a recent performing arts grad, and together with our third intern, Maha, we became best friends. Helena and I look strangely related, preternaturally youthful and alert, like the secret-keeping village children of a Grimms' fairy tale. She accompanied me to the name-change hearing as my witness and would later drive me to my top-surgery consultation.

Like Skylar, Helena somehow made the chores of transitioning *fun*. Having hamburgers and milkshakes with her and Maha later at our favorite lunch joint, I realized I wasn't as "behind" as I thought. In fact, at that moment I was right where I wanted to be.

✦ ✦ ✦

The courthouse in West Hartford was a generous half mile from my mom's door. I don't even think I told her the date, only that I was pursuing a hearing. As Helena and I strolled down Farmington Avenue, I felt a tinge of guilt color our otherwise carefree afternoon. I felt sad, and a little paranoid.

After the judge rebuked me for keeping my Social Security number on my phone and signed my probate orders, Helena took a picture of me holding them up in a folder outside.

It's sunny out, a perfect day, and I'm dressed too preppy, khakis and a polo. In the background, a man intrudes to pour a bucket of water on a sidewalk spill.

✦ ✦ ✦

My work as "Donald Collins" had only just begun. The probate order opened the door to the *real business*, starting with a new Social Security card and continuing to this day with a passport I have yet to correct.

My wallet's makeover thinned it out. Each document requires separate paperwork and, usually, a fee. Insurance, bank cards, driver's license, passport, school ID and e-mail—everything has a process. When friends asked me about the wayward "F" marker on my license, I told them the truth: I just got tired.

In fact, I recently changed my gender marker when I switched my driver's license to California. After a humiliatingly useless first visit to the DMV, I was forced to have a doctor fill out a form confirming my gender as "male" and my transition as "complete" before they would assign me that tiny "M."

"Do you have any letter to prove this?" the clerk had asked me upon noticing my application said "male" while my passport said otherwise.

"Only my life," I replied.

✦ ✦ ✦

A few months after my name-change court date, I returned, on the radar, to West Hartford and sat for a family dinner at my grandmother's. We all gave it our awkward best. My name rang strangely in everyone's mouths, like a code word.

Donnie is enjoying Boston. *Donnie* is going out with friends tonight.

Unbeknownst to me at the time, there was already another "Donnie" in my family, a cousin of my mother's who was a fighter pilot. My mom had hoped for a more gender-neutral name for me, or a boy's name she liked better. "Hayden" maybe, or "Ian." If I had been "born a boy," she had planned to name me "Russell," which I briefly considered adopting. I dabbled with a derivative of my birth middle name, but ultimately decided I wanted a clean break. I can't really explain how I settled on "Donald," only that the movie *Donnie Darko* probably had nothing to do with it.

In the swing of the 2016 election season, I remind myself of the good Donalds: Glover, Antrim, Sutherland, Faison, Westlake, Duck. Sure, there are a weird slew of serial killers with that first name, but then we've got Donald David Dixon Ronald O'Connor, best known for his role as Cosmo Brown in *Singing in the Rain*. Three of my best friends' dads are named Donald.

✦ ✦ ✦

Although I originally stuck with the nickname "Donnie," I now prefer "Donald." I like its vintage and the way my friends say it. I like that it has fewer search-engine results, fewer embarrassing photos. I like that it's kind of a new start within a new start.

My mom noticed the change in my e-mail signatures and asked about it. I was surprised when she did, even though we talk about so much now; the issue still seemed immortalized with a kind of parental revulsion.

"I can never call you 'Donnie,'" she had once said, weeping in the den. "I can never call you 'my son.'"

Now, as I plan a trip to the East Coast, she says, "Donald! It'll be so nice to have you home."

A Story Exchange

✦ ✦ ✦

A collection of first-person accounts from a wide range
of parents, transgender people under thirty,
and advocates. All interviews in this section were conducted
and compiled by Mary and Donald Collins. Where noted,
names and places have been changed to protect the privacy
of those subjects who asked not to be identified.

Parent Story Exchange

Mary Collins

No One Way

Not all people who transition from one gender to another embrace every possible surgery and medication. Not all families of transgender children are either fully on board or opposed to what a transition might entail.

Instead, we sit at a roundtable with no clear start or end, some children happy to simply shift their names and pronouns, while others choose aggressive surgeries. Some parents reject the entire process, while others feel comfortable with at least a portion of what their child plans to do to transition.

We need a new language that reflects those of us sitting at the roundtable. Right now, even the best-intentioned organizations and individuals speak in ways that feel like insider conversations among those who understand and agree with the group.

Imagine if at some point early in our experiences with Donald's transition someone had sat us down and asked:

Donald, are you scared? *Yes.*
Mary, are you scared? *Yes.*
Donald, do you agree with your mom's viewpoint on your
     transition? *No.*
Mary, do you agree with all that Donald's doing to transition? *No.*

Donald, are you afraid your mother will no longer love you? *Yes.*
Mary, are you afraid your child will leave you and no longer love
you? *Yes.*

Look at all of that shared fear just sitting there for both to see. Simply
acknowledging this common ground could have led to more empathy,
which is where our book project has brought us. In the end, we would
not be saying to each other, "Just get it!" Instead, we would be saying, "Please don't leave me" and "How can we understand each other
better?"

To repair, families need to see there is a range of paths that can lead
to reconciliation and healing. If one group does not offer you the right
answer, keep searching. There are so many parents and transgender
people out there with so many points of view and all sorts of facilitators
with their own unique styles.

Somewhere, there's a chair waiting for you.

Finding Parents Willing to Share Their Stories

She takes my call or e-mail but then says no, she does not want to be
interviewed. He apologizes. They are all afraid. I assure them they do
not have to be identified; all I need is their story so we can share it with
other parents going through similar tensions and trauma.

I was lucky with my first attempt, but after that I sent out more
than twenty e-mails and made half a dozen pleading phone calls before
I coaxed another parent to share how he/she felt about what happened
to their family when their child told them he/she/it was transgender.
We wanted a wide range of voices: immigrants, economically disad-
vantaged individuals, fathers, small-town families. But a third of the
people who agreed to be interviewed, ultimately changed their minds
and asked me to pull their text.

And, of course, the parents who feel most marginalized rarely show
up at support groups. PFLAG organizations nationwide offer outstanding help to gay, bi, lesbian, trans, and queer individuals, but such
groups are not as well set up to handle the angry or terrified parent.

Discussions usually focus on how to help a child through his or her transition and how to help the parent "get it." All of that is understandable, because the teens and college-age young adults going through a transition already face enormous pressures and obstacles. The counselors and medical professionals feel they must first focus on the young.

But if I wanted to find parents with a range of experiences, I could not rely solely on national LGBTQ organizations, because the pool of parents who work with those organizations is self-selecting. They are on board enough to go.

I was not.

Eight years ago, if a reporter had called me, I would not have agreed to tell my story. I would not have trusted anyone, because I felt every time I expressed any doubt, shared my grief, or felt shocked by the medical options available to my child, I was quieted, even spurned. An aggressively questioning parent like me did not fit into the available groups. I needed to get further along toward acceptance before I could sit in the circle. At one point, someone actually told me that, so it wasn't just that I assumed or "felt" that sentiment.

These many years later I realize I should have looked harder, because the majority of parents of transgender children—at least initially—feel more in line with how I felt at that time. At least 40 percent of transgender children wind up homeless at some point, which, to me, translates to mean that nearly half of all parents of trans children are so conflicted about what's going on that they are drowning.

There are not enough places right now for those parents. Many of them will come to fully embrace everything about their transgender child, others may just come to some satisfactory space where they agree to disagree and move back to what they love about each other. Those who do make this more positive journey are largely out there on their own right now. I seriously believe the homelessness rate for transgender youth can be cut in half with more support programs for conflicted parents. If they felt more respected, felt "heard," and weren't told to "get it" before they even know what "it" is, they might not become so afraid and enraged.

As one parent told me, to be asked to just go along with such a radical change is to "strip a person of their humanity."

The fundamental structure of the current support system for parents of trans children makes it extremely difficult to find parents who, for example, have tossed their kids out of the house. As I learned from interviews with parents, counselors, and individuals who work for nonprofits such as PFLAG, the mothers and fathers who feel the most alienated by the entire experience of having a trans child, and who probably need the most assistance, are the last to seek it out. They hunker down. They close out everyone, including their child.

I heard of one angry mother, who, rather than change her point of view about her child's decision to transition, accepted being ostracized by her entire extended family. I wanted to hear her story. I was lightly mocked by her family members for wanting to talk to her, as though by asking I was taking her side, and they found that offensive. I countered: But at some point she loved this child. Can't we find a way back for her, for the child?

I communicated via e-mail with someone still in contact with the woman but had no luck reaching her. All trust was gone. All hope was gone.

So, I do not have the story of a parent who chose to cut all ties with his or her child and kicked that child out of the house, thus leaving the child homeless, even though for at least 40 percent of families with transgender children, that is the story.

What I do have is an interview with a successful group facilitator whom many families credited with saving their children's lives, their marriages, and their home life. Libby McKnight offers a model for what can happen in group work for even the most conflicted parent.

Donald and I hope that our candid—often even pained—exchanges as parent and trans son will facilitate conversations that will draw a wider range of people to the table. For all those parents who feel they have lost so much, we hope this story exchange makes you feel a little less isolated and more motivated to seek help.

SOUTHERN CATHOLIC FAMILY
SEEKS MIDDLE GROUND

The father says he and his wife raised a "traditional family," with a dad who went off to work, a stay-at-home mom, and four children. They lived in the South, were active in their church, and placed their daughter in an all-girls' Catholic high school.

THE DAD
Leslie Becomes Larry

Leslie announced she was gay when she was twenty-two and living on her own after graduating college and taking a job. Around that time she was dressing, well, I guess you'd say pretty dour. Almost like a Chinese-worker-from-the-collective-farms kind of thing. There was definitely something different about her, but we weren't sure what.

Well, I'm a pretty religious guy. When Leslie disclosed that she was gay, I shared that God made us the way He did and you remain a child of God regardless of your orientation. The gay life-style is in contrast to how we live our lives, but it's in God's hands. It was not welcomed news, but we were prepared to learn more about what it meant.

The name and pronoun did not change during that first year.

When Leslie was twenty-three she sent us an extended e-mail announcing, "I am trans." Perhaps she felt it would be easier to communicate something with that much depth [by writing], that it was easier to get it across.

Now, that was a major change. My wife and I just didn't see it. I just didn't understand it. No doctor, counselor, teacher, family member, or coach ever suggested that there was something we were not seeing in Leslie. Then "Larry" started taking hormones.

He talked about wanting to be male. We were concerned whether he'd do surgery, and we didn't want him to rush into anything. Leslie/Larry has a lot of food allergies and issues, so we said, "Your body is stressed out. The hormones will add additional stress."

But then we found out she had already started hormones. Larry would share things with us after the thing had gone on for a while. Our counsel was not received.

In the e-mail Larry said, "You repressed me when my orientation began to emerge earlier." I felt that was a rationalization. The thought that there was a perception that we would not love Leslie enough that we'd want to repress her . . . [silence]

What's in a Name?

"Leslie Nicole" was my daughter's name. "Nicole" is a family name. . . . We lovingly gave our daughter her name. It meant a lot to me, and it was something really emotional to process [when Leslie changed her name to Larry and dropped "Nicole"].

And the pronouns are really difficult. My wife can't do it. Me, I can barely do it. I know Leslie knows we love him/her and we support him/her.

We generally dodge trying to say "he" or "she" in group settings. When people ask if we have kids, we still say three boys and a girl and leave it at that. Most people are satisfied with that and move on.

But we've been in the community a long time. We haven't shared it with a lot of people because Leslie has moved away. Our best friends know and recognize the stress on our family and offer support for Leslie and us.

It's definitely good that my wife and I have each other.

Mother and Father React Differently

My wife was at home. Raising the children was her life's work. I was there as well. I shared in that, but I worked outside the home.

She and I are taking this quite differently, partially because of our natures. When I wake up in the morning, I think there's a lot of good coming. When she wakes up in the morning, she worries about what will happen. She is so concerned what could happen if Leslie/Larry does surgeries.

There's been some communication between Leslie/Larry and my wife about whose "fault" this is, or if we did something wrong. I think God has his plan for us all and tend to look forward rather than back.

My wife and I have prayed together more and harder than in the past. We both gain strength from our faith. We continue to love and support Leslie. But it's so upsetting—the idea of her changing her body and shape, and perhaps going to surgery to alter her body. We want Leslie to be happy, to be healthy, to thrive. We shared this with Leslie.

We let *all* of our children know we do not completely agree with all of their choices and decisions.

I think the female is more thoughtful and really trying to process all of her emotions. How did this come about? How did this happen? We had someone we loved and perceived as a certain way, and now they are different. It's much harder on my wife. Males tend to let things roll off of them more easily. Life goes on. Now what?

My wife sometimes has arguments with Leslie. She'll bring up that Leslie is a relatively young person, and that when she [the mother] was that age she thought she was right about a lot of things and now she knows she wasn't and, hmmm, maybe it wasn't such a good idea.

Seeking Help Proves Difficult

We went to [Chicago] to see Leslie and to see her counselor. It was a gay rights clinic. But the counselor saw it as her job to help Larry with his/her transition instead of answering our questions or even questioning if it was the right thing. So that did not go well.

This idea that a parent has to be completely supportive or

opposed to the transition is polarizing. It strips a person of their humanity to assume they must fall in line. Love is complicated. Life is complicated. You must process it in your own way.

Very Little Middle Ground

I find there's very little middle ground when you talk to people or read literature intended to help. They say you're hateful if you are not supportive or bad if you do support this "bad" behavior. Get in line. Fall behind them. That's the attitude. So we need to find a middle ground.

It's been comforting talking with you.

MEXICAN-AMERICAN MOTHER, RESISTANT FATHER, A TRANS SON

M., the Barajases' teenaged trans son, first mustered up the courage to talk with his mother about his growing sense that he was not a girl after he saw a video from an episode of The Oprah Winfrey Show *that featured transgender teens. After years of dressing like a boy, preferring the company of other boys, and hearing himself referred to as a "tomboy," M. realized that he was transgender.*

At first he did not come right out and use that term with his mother, but instead talked about the kids in the video.

"Isn't it sad that the kids can't just be themselves," he said to her.

"I said, 'Yeah,'" Mrs. Barajas recalls but then admits that she thought her tomboyish daughter was just being sensitive to the struggles of others.

Pronouns and Body Parts: United States vs. Overseas

By sixth grade, M. wasn't talking about other kids anymore but about himself; his mother knew that her daughter no longer wanted to present as female, did want to change her name and pronouns and, perhaps down the line, even more. M.'s father, who often travels overseas, did not know what was going on for some time. When M. did come out to him, he lamented the loss of his daughter and dug in about not switching to the new pronouns.

Mrs. Barajas says, "I did not share these things with my husband. He was more removed from it all because he travels so much for work. M. was afraid to tell him. He feared rejection."

But then the family had to travel overseas for two years, and Mrs. Barajas suggested that M. start their new life as a boy using the new name at the new school right from the start. A year later, M. moved to a different school and this time registered as a boy and started to bind his breasts. The father had to accept that his daughter was officially registered as a boy at school.

"At home there was a lot of yelling and crying," Mrs. Barajas recalls. "I told my husband not to negate M., but he [the husband] felt M. was too young to know what he was doing and felt it was more of a phase. He did not want M. doing something irreversible on 'his watch.'

"So as a family, we are not navigating things all that well. We have a lot of big fights and no resolutions."

While overseas for two years, they were in a country that does not allow "blockers," which prevent a preteen from going through puberty. But M. requested to take them as soon as they returned to the States.

"I never questioned whether or not M. should use blockers, but my husband did," Mrs. Barajas said. "So when I communicated with my husband [about this issue], I used three steps: I make him aware; I wait for him to deal with it in his mind; we have a conversation about things.

"It was all very slow. It took eighteen months for him to just process the name and pronoun change. [He] initially went nuts [about the blockers], but then mulled it over and said okay.

"So M. started blockers and plans to have top surgery this summer."

Visits to Mexico

"I am Mexican and raised Catholic. In my family we never talked about anything, so I said that I would say everything when I became a parent. I really value open communication with my children. I worried that my extended family may not accept M., but they have. Everyone is supportive. We go to Mexico every year, and I reassure [M.] no one will harm him. I must be *on* and fully aware and 'correct' my family when they do not use the right words."

Striving for a Unified Response as a Couple

When asked why did she assume her husband should "get on board," Mrs. Barajas said, "I am not going to live M.'s life; he must do that for himself and on his own terms and not feel bad about it. So [my husband] needs M. to live his life as he sees fit.

"In the end, the thing that freaked me out the most was not that I 'lost' a daughter but that I saw the pain that was coming, and that was hard for me. I could see there would be a big crash."

UNCONDITIONAL SUPPORT

Lisa is the mother of Robin Ezra (nicknamed Puck). Puck, formerly named Lily, transitioned to the use of "they" as a pronoun and had a name change in college. While sitting in a coffee shop in Connecticut with me, Lisa reflected on her child's transition to a gender-fluid, more masculine identity. A tall, intelligent woman who spent a lot of her professional life in music journalism, Lisa tried to embrace and celebrate her child's transition from the start.

LISA

Level of Acceptance

If their [Puck's] parents do not accept them, then how can they find acceptance from other people? I just felt it was my responsibility to support Puck's transition. We're very close.

They're still the same person. They have the same interests; we talk about the same things and still laugh about the same things. It was not always a smooth transition, but I do not feel that they are a different person.

Pronouns and Body Parts

The language piece has been the hardest because we had to switch pronouns. (Puck currently uses "they" or "he," depending on the setting.) The nickname "Puck" happened in high school, and in college "Lily" was dropped. It took a while to get used to it because I was so attached to the name. That was my kid's name. They were named after my husband's grandmother, an artist and very cool person. But we got used to Puck. It's a *Midsummer Night's Dream* reference, and Puck loves Shakespeare.

The legal name change just happened a few weeks ago [Puck had graduated college just a few months prior to the interview]. They didn't have a license and weren't confident showing any ID. When we went to get a nondriving license, they cried. "Why do I need an ID with my old name and a legal gender marker on it?" they asked. Everything legal is always a big emotional upheaval. I agreed that it would be helpful to just legally change their name to one they chose, so this past fall we did that. I think the name change helped me as much as Puck. Now when people say, "How's Lily?" I say that's not their name anymore; it's Robin Ezra. It helps me. I don't always want to give long explanations.

Hormones from an NYC Clinic

Puck took a semester at Sarah Lawrence College to participate in a writing program, and while near New York City, they went to clinic in Manhattan and began hormone therapy.

My husband and I were afraid that any medical complications could distract from schoolwork. We just wanted them to get through school and deal with transitional issues later. But being the independent person that they are, they couldn't wait. We were scared at first, as we were not sure of the side effects of the testosterone, but it has been going well so far.

My husband went with Puck to visit [the clinic] with Puck's permission. He felt that [the medical staff] did not spend a lot of time with him, and he wasn't sure if they [the doctors] answered his questions, but a doctor did speak to him. They admitted that they did not know all the long-term effects of hormone therapy, but assured him [the dad] that they would be doing blood-work periodically to make sure hormone levels were where they needed to be.

Endings and Beginnings

I do not have to kill or mourn the past. Actually we were looking at old videos of when [Puck was] a little kid and laughing, and we still have some childhood pictures around the house. I am happy about that. I had eighteen years of a daughter (or so I thought), and it was great. No one is asking me to deny that.

Disclosure

Sometimes I'll see people in the grocery store [who knew Puck in high school] and they ask how "Lily" is. I have to think fast: How well do I know this person? How much do they want to know? I just make snap judgments, and also I must decide if we have time [to get into a discussion]. Sometimes I'll give a little five-minute account of Puck's transition. Some are confused, but most people have always known that our kid was unique. Puck was even voted most unique in their high school yearbook.

Protecting Your Child

We lived through 9/11. We lived just blocks away [from the World Trade Center]. Puck was eight. As a parent I've been through some really scary stuff: how to get my kid through a terrorist attack and through to the other side in terms of dealing with emotional issues.

[A few years after, at age twelve, Puck was diagnosed with scoliosis and had to have back surgery.]

I think Puck's taking control of their transition has enabled them to have more of a sense of overall control.

I can't always protect my kid from a dangerous world, but at least I can be as supportive as possible.

COUPLE FINDS A WAY TO WORK IN TANDEM

Most couples I spoke with did not fare well as they navigated a child's transition, but the mother of one trans son from the Mid-Atlantic region talked about how important it was that she and her husband went through everything together, including the support groups, where few husbands/fathers ever came and certainly rarely stayed.

Their daughter began showing signs of discomfort with her gender as early as age four, when some mornings, Judy says, her daughter would wake up and exclaim, "I'm going to be a boy today!" At age seven, their daughter felt incredibly stressed about buying a dress for First Communion.

By college, C. had changed her name to T., began using male pronouns, and underwent top surgery.

THE MOM

Attending Counseling Sessions as a Couple

My husband and I both agreed T. was different, but we were clueless about what was happening. We went to a support group. At that point T. was about nineteen.

The first session was awful. There were lots of older men transitioning to women, and they didn't pass well as women. So scary. Others had a lot of emotional issues. Luckily we kept going. At first we just didn't understand. I did a lot of research. My husband was more skeptical about our daughter transitioning and the physical changes, but he came around.

Men don't feel comfortable in support groups. [With] one couple, the husband came once but then did not come again. It's really hard what they are saying, so it's hard for a parent to hear. At the time, we wanted to believe that this was a phase.

But the support group really helped.

At the time, it was all really stressful, but I think we're probably better off for it [as a couple]. We're back to the same place now. [My husband] would go to the support group, and no other men would go, so that really helped.

It was all really hard at first, but when we saw the change and our new "son" became so outgoing and friendly, when we saw that it made a world of difference, well, there was no question at all that we did the right thing. I did not feel that way a few years ago, but my husband and I feel the same way about that now. It's been a good thing, not easy, but a good thing.

Response to C. Coming Out as T.

T. came out to us together as a couple. He was eighteen. He had first said he was attracted to girls and brought his first girlfriend home, but then a year later he said he was trans. He came out to his counselor first before the family. He'd been involved in an LBGT group and was even mentoring some people.

When we first found out, I was like "Oh my God, can you make your life any harder?" We were proud of him for helping others but also worried about his safety during transition. His name was published in the school newspaper and showed up online after he appeared in an assembly before the school. Once at a party, he was confronted by a group of male students. The students harassed him and wanted to know if he was male or female. He left the party and they followed him. Fortunately he got home okay.

There were signs very early on. She wanted to be like her older brother and sometimes woke up and said, "I'm going to be a boy today!"

I remember a PE coach telling me, "She's so strong. I mean really strong. She should do professional weightlifting."

Now, my husband is tall, six foot two, and athletic, and the kids have always been athletic. She did look very much like a girl, but she went from lacrosse to track and was on track for just a few weeks and did shotput and discus and went to the states in discus the first time she tried it. She participated in swimming, soccer, basketball, volleyball, and field hockey also.

In high school she still used her given name. She was very depressed her junior year, so we sent her to a counselor. She had no close friends because she didn't feel she could open up to anyone her age. I thought she had body-image problems because she never felt comfortable in female clothing. The doctor said, "She's not developing normally for puberty," but added that it was nothing to worry about.

Names and Pronouns

He changed his name from C. to T. His [given] middle name was J., my mom's, and she died, so I was really sad about that. My husband was actually angry about the name change, that T. had done it without talking to him. We accepted the name change after a few months, back in 2010, and [have] used the new name since.

Once T. shifted the pronouns and his name, he was so happy, so we were like, "Okay, we have to be supportive." He hadn't been happy since puberty, so this was the first time in six years. I was sad about taking photos down at his request. I realized I could have a photographer take a new photo of the transitioned T. in a suit to add a photo to my display of my children's graduation photos, and that helped me feel better.

T.'s Depression

[My husband and I] both talked about T.'s depression and were scared to death he'd kill himself in college. We did not want him in such a desperate situation, so our main goal—both of us—was to be supportive. We realized we had to be supportive. Right or wrong, we had to give T. that support.

T.'s Decision to Have Surgery

T. started thinking about surgery in his junior year [of college]. His talk about removing his breasts really freaked us out. We found a counselor down the street, so we went to see her. My husband and I both went. She was supporting T. She asked us, "So what's the worst thing that could happen?"

It would cost money. [Insurance did not cover it.] We agreed to loan T. the money, and he has to pay it back. I didn't want to give the money and then if he came back later and was unhappy about it [the decision for surgery] and asked, "Why did you support that?"—well, I didn't want to be responsible for that, so we decided we would tell him that he had to pay back the money. But my husband and I thought we would forgive the debt later, and we did.

We went to an event in Philly, and people there were showing their scars from the surgery, and we actually felt better.

So T. had chest surgery just prior to his senior year. He did it down in Florida because there was a doctor down there he wanted to use. I went to be with him. Actually a friend came with me, not my husband. It was fine. By then I was ready for it. I did feel he was old enough to make his own decisions, and I wanted to help him. The counselor kept saying, "It's his decision to know his own gender."

T. has talked about doing more surgery but isn't sure.

Siblings Respond

Our older daughter is in the theater and knew a lot of gay friends but not anyone trans. She questioned if [T.] was old enough to make these decisions. My [other] son is in a fraternity. He was afraid of being embarrassed at his wedding. He was engaged to be married and all of his friends knew T. as a girl. So he freaked out. But he had a great friend in high school who was like, "Don't you want to hang onto your relationship with your sister?"

He didn't end up getting married, so we didn't have to deal with all of it.

Community Response

The neighbors have been very supportive. One of them, who is not religious but a spiritual person, gave me a God Box. I write down a worry and put it in the box, and I let God handle it. This was a great help for me to let go of anxiety and cope.

I was worried about my sister [a devout Christian], but she and her family have been very kind to T. She doesn't understand his situation but accepts him.

Biggest Fear

My biggest fear is that T. will never find a partner, someone special to share his life with.

Final Thoughts

Parents need to stay open-minded with their child when they discuss transition. We kept wanting to slow down the process, but T. reminded us that he had been struggling for years with his identity. It was not a spur-of-the-moment decision for him. I reminded T. that it was new to us and he needed to be patient with us. We struggled to change the pronouns and name for a year, but T. was patient with us. Today, I see his old photo and it seems odd. I now see this happy, healthy son. Not that life is perfect, but our struggles are now typical parent/son relationship issues, like "Why did you buy a motorcycle?"

WHEN TRANS TEENS ALSO HAVE MENTAL HEALTH ISSUES

Roxane Orgill and her husband, Conrad, adopted two children, a girl and a boy, through a domestic agency. The older child, Charlotte, came out in her teens as transgender. She now goes by Charlie and presents as male. But, as Roxane makes clear in her interview, the family first had to wrestle with their child's mental health issues and never even knew to look for or address the transgender issue.

Research shows that transgender youth are more apt to struggle with mental health issues than the cisgender population, in particular anxiety and depression, though the percentage that is diagnosed as bipolar is not significantly higher than that in the cisgender population, according to recent studies. Roxane advises all parents to address mental health issues before transgender issues via therapy, medication, and whatever else is required.

ROXANE
Daughter Struggles with Mental Illness

Charlotte was a tomboy but not excessively so. She liked knights and liked stuffed animals and was artistic. She started having some trouble in school, so we put her in a private progressive Christian school, which had tiny classes. But around eighth grade things started to get rough. She was throwing things, sharp pencils, and they didn't want her there. She was always difficult to raise.

We used a therapist to help, but we decided that the high school in town was not a good match. Instead we moved to the Bronx/Riverdale area in New York and had Charlotte go to a local school. I figured it would be more diverse, more types of kids. Her old school had like 160 kids, and this school had like 700. But it was a really bad move. By December we had lost her.

She was very defiant, doing drugs, and just doing poorly.
At one point she took a large quantity of Melatonin, a sleep aid.
It wasn't really a suicide attempt; she was trying to calm herself
down.

At this point we moved her to therapeutic high schools—four
schools in four years—and she was diagnosed as bipolar. These
schools had treatment programs, each one a little less restrictive
than the next.

Making Decisions About Charlotte's Care as a Couple

We had several terrible decision-making moments, especially right
after the pill [overdose] incident. [My husband, Conrad,] felt she
should be home, but I said no. He thought it was cruel to send her
away. I am a writer and work at home a lot, and I was the one who
would have had to deal with her. That was inconceivable to me.
I couldn't handle it. I said, "You try it." He said, "I can't because
I'm the primary breadwinner."

So all of the failings in our marriage came out.

[Around the time Charlotte was twelve], I started going to
a therapist who worked with the family through me. She met
Charlotte—I think once—and Conrad came a few times. He felt
so much better afterwards.

The gender issue was still not in the open yet. Each time she
graduated from a program, she would come home and we'd use
the therapist as the middle piece, an anchor. [My husband and I]
realized we could work through this as a couple.

Charlotte Tells Her Family She Is Transgender

At one point a therapist did talk about gender dystopia, . . . but the
main diagnosis was bipolar disorder. [Charlotte] went on meds.
We didn't know what to do; she was so unmanageable. She was
out of control.

She did say, "I'm gay."

I just said that sexuality can be a really fluid thing, so I was supportive and not surprised. I didn't care that much. I was mainly concerned with trying to keep her safe. We had no other gay person in the [extended] family.

We were all home in the summer, and at dinner when Charlotte said she had something she couldn't wait to tell us.

"I am transgender. I want to live as a man."

She cried.

My husband, the lawyer, was totally cool; [the brother] sat there wide-eyed. I was in shock. After all of this work and effort, now this.

Now I see that for the [previous] three years, Charlotte had been wearing boxers, guy's jeans, shirts—gradually shifting her clothing. That was the first big sign. We fought about it. [The boarding school had a dress code, so it sort of hid the progression from the family's view.]

But for me to go from the clothing and dressing like a boy and binding [her breasts] to being transgender was just a huge step, a huge leap. I mean, to be going on hormones . . . [She] had already found a doctor. Now I look back and I feel is it really no different, but at the time it was huge. I couldn't even think about surgery.

Charlie was very gentle with me. As a family we were in a good place to communicate about all of this; we were much further along because of all of the therapy. I did not feel she was acting out; this was not impulsive like in the past. So both me and my husband took this very seriously. It was a relief to [truly believe] this was not an impulsive act. I wanted it to go away but . . .

For a few months I did hope she'd change her mind, but I had learned to be more flexible.

Ongoing Mental Health Issues

We were focused so strongly on getting [Charlotte] the right meds and therapy so she could go to school and eventually leave the therapeutic boarding schools—not to come home but to go to a normal boarding school. We tried a regular boarding school, but she only lasted three weeks. She started throwing things and terrifying students. They made us get her immediately.

[Eventually] Charlotte graduated [from another school]. I really researched things and found a program in West Virginia that offers work and support for those still dealing with mental illness. I was trying to get her into a world where it would be possible for her to develop skills she needs to work independently. That [program] has been fantastic.

Balancing Mental Health Care with Gender Transition

Why couldn't she wait until she was twenty-five or something? But no, she had made her mind up. You know, once they make up their mind to go through with the transition to get on the hormones, there's no stopping it. But a doctor was required and a lot of blood work. She's on lithium [for bipolar disorder]. What a combo.

The program [she was in] still housed her with two girls; the guys were a rough bunch, but the girls were okay. But now she . . . he . . . has made further progress and is sharing a house with a guy. She . . . he . . . my Charlie . . . is in a program with a therapist, a psychiatrist, and life coach, and there's huge support. [Charlie] doesn't drive because of his focus issues, but [coming out as transgender] has had a calming effect on his moods. Not sure if it's also just maturing.

Both [challenges] have been tremendously difficult. I wanted a normal daughter. But at least with the bipolar it hit young, so we had some control because Charlotte was a minor and we could treat it. It became a project. As a couple we agreed to put all of our resources into it. Transgender . . . It's not an illness. You're in shock. You don't "treat" it. If he's of age and it's his decision, well . . . but if [your child] is a minor, it's not so easy.

I spoke with a trans man who had therapy who told me his family had turned him out of their lives. "You don't believe this now," he said, "but you could have a whole new relationship with your child, an even better one."

That really gave me hope. We achieved our flexibility after all of this therapy, so I was open to it. That's cool. I could see [the new relationship] happening.

BUILDING TRUST AS A FACILITATOR: LIBBY MCKNIGHT

In an effort to find subjects for my parent roundtable, I approached many organizations devoted to helping gay, bi, lesbian, queer, and transgender people. One facilitator in particular, from the Mid-Atlantic region, Libby, stood out as someone who had a knack for winning the trust of conflicted parents. Again and again, even though most of the parents who heard about my project through her did not want to have their story in *At the Broken Places*, they did credit Libby and her group with "saving them."

After speaking with her at length, I thought it was clear that her strongest attributes as a group facilitator were empathy and openness. She had gone through a huge change with her own husband, S., who had come out as transgender about eighteen years into their marriage. Libby had always known that her husband liked cross-dressing, but after he became involved with a cross-dressing theater group, it was clear that something much more profound was at work.

"This is who I am," he told her. "I feel that I am really a woman."

"I had had an experience with my best friend, who had been horribly abused as a very young child," Libby recalled, "and he told me that he did not want to be touched. Of course when he said this, I wanted to hug him, but instead I stepped away. He was so relieved.

"That was one of my first experiences with doing what someone else needed me to do, so I was able to tell my husband that I got it and I could accept that expressing his feminine side was truly who he was."

They've been married for thirty-two years. S. transitioned in 2002 and had sexual reassignment surgery in 2005.

Libby joined a PFLAG Trans Families support group in Maryland within the first year after her husband began to transition. After going for a few years, and serving as a substitute facilitator, she noticed that a lot of the families and couples were coming from Virginia, so she launched a Northern Virginia chapter. She stepped easily into the facilitator role thanks to her training as a social worker and other courses in leadership. She also works as a professional sign-language interpreter and does quite a bit of volunteer work with PFLAG, her progressive Methodist Church, and Landmark Worldwide, an organization that provides courses in personal realization.

The entire time I spoke with her and heard others speak about her, I sensed that degrees and previous experience were just a small reason why Libby excelled at reaching conflicted parents. Unlike some of the other nonprofit support groups I'd been in contact with, in Libby's, she made it clear that she wanted to support the family and not only the young person in transition. She feels, and models for the group, an acceptance of where each individual may be in the complicated process of understanding what's going on.

"I acknowledge that the parents need the group as much as the kids. That's what our group is for!" she says. "Oh, yeah, I make it clear that we are here to support the whole family, and trans folks are welcome to come, but the focus is not on them; it is on the parents, spouses, and other family, and their experiences.

"I have been a bit stubborn with PFLAG because I call my group a *support* group, while they call it a community group, but it means something to me to emphasize the word 'support.'"

I told her that the more "community" focused approach made me feel more like a person who did not have the right passport, because I questioned so many things. As I saw it, the community setup was meant to create a firewall of support for the people in transition. By under-scoring support for all the participants in a family processing a son or daughter in transition, Libby was making a subtle but important ad-justment in emphasis.

Despite her popularity as a facilitator, she acknowledges that about half the parents who come to the group for the first time never come back.

"I do worry that people don't come back, because as facilitators we so respect trans people and it's so important to express that, but many of the parents are simply not ready to hear all of this."

She pauses after reflecting on this and says, "Maybe I should send them an e-mail and just thank them for coming. I don't do that, and maybe I should."

We both agree that the most conflicted parents don't even show up, and those who do are often mustering all the courage they can because they love their child.

"I think it's important that people come when they are ready to come. Don't have them come if they are not ready to be there. Give them something like your book [*At the Broken Places*], ask them to read it, and make it clear that this *is* happening and you need to reflect on what you want to do next to show your love for your kid or partner."

Libby said that one of her more stressful encounters was when a very quiet, meek trans woman brought her wife, a highly opinionated woman, to the group when she, the wife, wasn't ready to talk about support.

"That wife just started pounding the table and yelled, 'When will it be my turn to get what I want?'

"I told her that I understood how upsetting this was for her [that her husband wanted to transition to being a woman], but there was nothing I could do to change that. I let her vent. It happened that there were no other folks attending that meeting, but if that had happened in the general group with other parents or spouses attending, it would have been hugely disruptive."

After more than fifteen years working with families, transgender young people, and spouses or partners, Libby says the most noticeable change she's seen is that more parents of teens are showing up. When she first started going to the group in Maryland, most of the trans people were in their fifties and sixties, and were coming out because their parents had passed and they just didn't want to wait anymore. Now, more and more young people seem to feel free to push for a transition during or even before puberty.

As a parent, I wish I had had a facilitator like Libby, who showcased skills that I know would have helped me, including

- Empathy, rather than judgment, for whatever stage in the process a parent might be in
- Championing a whole-family approach that does not hyperfocus on the needs of the teen in transition at the expense of the entire family
- Accepting that at meetings some parents will sit there in silence, never put on a nametag, and may never return
- Acknowledging that most support groups need to reach out more to conflicted parents
- Providing support as the primary goal in whatever shape and form that might take, rather than telling someone to just "get it"

Near the close of the interview I asked Libby what she might have said to me and Donald when he was pressing for top surgery and hormones, and I was vehemently opposed.

She reflected for a few seconds before answering.

"If I had faced your scenario, I would have said that I respect your right as a mom to say, 'You cannot use my insurance and you need to do this on your own dime because I just don't trust everything that's going on,' and to Donald I would have said, 'I completely understand why you feel a deep need to do the surgeries.'"

An open mind, a fair hearing, balanced advice. That seems like a good recipe for repairing families who face unique pressures when a child transitions from one gender to another.

Transgender Youth and Professionals Story Exchange

Donald Collins

Getting Perspective

This interview series intends to provide supplementary trans-related perspectives across identity boundaries. The voices included in these sections have established themselves as gender activists, leaders, and/or qualified professionals.

After I came out in high school, building a supportive community took time and a lot of self-education. I worked hard to use the resources available to me, whether it was the Internet, a support group, or a therapist. I remember the Google-storm of my first week with the word "trans" and being overwhelmed by the sheer amount of conflicting and incomplete information.

Understanding the complex issues trans people face, the inconsistencies of the medical system, and the sheer variety of sex and gender expression out there brings necessary context to my own experiences. I wouldn't have made it without friends, mentors, and good health-care professionals to guide me.

Central to each of these interviews is the issue of "family" support. Some of the people interviewed faced (and still face) strained or negative relationships with their parents and other relatives. While others may come out on better terms, no family dynamic is perfect, and other forms of prejudice and discrimination are not erased by a happy home.

These interviews also seek to provide anchorage for families who don't know what to expect or who feel unprepared. If you are concerned for the future of your trans child, sometimes it helps to see trans people living and working in the world. If you are unable to see *your* child as trans, then maybe hearing from someone *else's* trans child will adjust your vision. If you are confused about new terminology, maybe seeing these words in context will better impress their meanings.

Many LGBTQ people lead full and loving lives without any connection with their family. Some families leverage trans children financially or emotionally to keep them in the closet. Trans people may cut themselves off by choice to protect themselves, while others may be iced out, kicked out, or both. There are those who have positive relationships with one parent but not the other, or with a sibling but not their parents. There are those like me who experienced rough patches but maintain contact.

It's clear that we are reaching a turning point in trans education and advocacy. We recognize that family and home life can provide a substantial source of stress for trans people coming out at any age. According to the findings of the National Transgender Discrimination Survey, around 57 percent of the more than six thousand trans respondents experienced some level of family rejection. Among those who reported rejection, homelessness was nearly three times higher, and other negative factors, like suicide risk and substance abuse, also increased.

As the attorney I spoke to put it, "Human rights is a better framework for trans rights, because it's about basic survival. It's about things that you deserve as a human being. You deserve to be loved, you deserve to be safe, you deserve to have food and shelter." I'd like to think all parents can agree with that.

The NTDS's recommendations for family-life issues demand a collective commitment to overhauling outdated legal and medical policies, and widening the availability of educational resources. Parents need to communicate and self-educate; social workers and family courts need specific training on the risks facing trans youth; families need access to qualified therapists and counselors.

There isn't a quick fix. I don't think my situation is representative of most trans people's, insofar as my reconnection with my mother goes. I don't think it would be fair to say, "We did it; so can you!" That's not what this book is about.

A fairer summary would go something like, "We barely did it; here's what we learned."

ASK A LAWYER: DRU

Dru Levasseur is a white trans guy in his early forties who is a trans activist and attorney. He grew up in New England and is now based in New York City.

The following are select excerpts from our conversation, which covered his coming-out, the beginnings of his activism, and his leadership on the LGBTQ legal front.

What is your personal conception of "gender"?

DRU: One of the things that I've realized is truly important is that most people are raised with this idea of "binary gender." That you hold up the baby, you look at their genitals, you pick one of two boxes. In my work as a transgender rights attorney, I've realized that there's this gap in understanding. There's this idea that there's this so-called "real" or "biological" sex that is what you *really* are, and that any other identity is intangible, that it's "in your head."

I, myself, needed to expand my understanding that sex is actually more complicated than that moment at birth, or just genitals and chromosomes. It's very helpful to our legal work to bring in actual experts to show that "here are all of the different factors that go into a determination of sex."

When I'm talking to a room of people, most folks in the room assume that they know what gender they are, and they think that all of those different categories line up. But everybody might have variations, like some people have different levels of hormones than other people. The bottom line is, the one thing that medical science shows, is that the one determining factor out of all of those things is the self-identity. Self-identity is actually rooted in biology. It is who people *are*; it is rooted in their brains.

Dru and I spoke at length about House Bill 2, a controversial North Carolina bill signed into law in March 2016. Like many anti-trans laws, the bill's logic claims to be rooted in an immutable understanding of male/female biology.

HB-2, also called the "bathroom bill," stipulates that people must use the bathroom that corresponds with their "biological sex" or the gender marker on their birth certificate. The bill passed quickly—within a single day—and divisive reactions reared just as quickly. Democratic legislators walked out in protest during the vote and soon filed for repeal. Opponents picketed the legislative building and decried the bill on Twitter, while celebrities and businesses canceled events and plans in the state.

So why did it pass in the first place?

Supporters argued that HB-2 prevents "men in dresses" from preying on women and children, falling back on the concept that trans women are really men in disguise. And not just men but pedophiles and criminals. Far from serving as a safety precaution, HB-2 instead discriminates openly against those who may not fit its poorly defined notion of "sex" and who already face harassment and violence in public spaces.

"Violence statistics are very real against *all* women, especially trans women of color," Dru said. "And, you know, targeting trans people and combining those two ideas is extremely harmful and inaccurate."

Why are we so adamant about having people "look" two specific ways [male or female]?

DRU: I think it gets back to HB-2 and all of these anti-trans bills. This hysteria that's happening is really tapping into and taking advantage of the lack of public education around who transgender people are. And I think that our culture, our society, understands gender in very simple terms. When somebody's born, they have to fit in a box, one box or the other.

So out of that ignorance and power struggle over gender control come these laws that mandate using the restroom based on "biological sex." [Legislators] don't even know what they're talking about because, as I said earlier, gender identity is, in fact, "biological" and the most important factor in determining someone's sex!

Dru pointed out that those who face the most distress in bathrooms are people who are read as gender-variant or non-conforming. So, HB-2 specifically targets members of the trans or queer community who *look different*, including those who don't easily fit into those gender boxes or who don't have the resources to transition medically. It affects *anyone* who doesn't meet the strict standards of masculine/feminine gender stereotypes, regardless of whether they are trans.

Both Dru and I recognize that we no longer read as gender-ambiguous, though we shared stories of bad bathroom experiences from earlier in our transitions.

Dru recalled that the last time he was accosted in a bathroom, he was trying to use the women's room in an airport and still legally had an "F" on his driver's license. He was "arm-barred" on his neck from entering by a woman who said, "This is the ladies' room!"

In high school, I went to use the boys' bathroom shortly after my coming-out senior year. A teacher deliberately followed me inside the otherwise empty restroom to yell, "Is there a girl in here?"

After speaking about bathrooms for a while, Dru summed up: "Just use the f-king restroom and leave each other alone!"

It's one thing to experience discrimination or anxiety firsthand, but communicating it to others can be difficult.

In an April 2016 study published in the journal *Science*, authors David Broockman and Joshua Kalla found that having canvassers go door-to-door in Miami and speaking with random constituents for ten to fifteen minutes noticeably reduced anti-trans prejudice for a period of time. Canvassers were both cis and trans people, which suggests another important factor: this kind of advocacy doesn't necessarily have to be the burden of queer people alone.

In Dru's work, whether litigating or speaking, he is often people's first point of contact with an openly trans person. He possesses a potent combination of professional training *and* personal experience.

Do you find that the effectiveness of this kind of person-to-person communication really holds true in your work?

DRU: The reality is that when people have a human connection to any community, they realize [the other person is also] a person, just like them, and it really makes a difference. And I think that's the gap. We saw that with the success of Harvey Milk encouraging gay people to come out, because once people started coming out, people realized, "Oh, my next-door neighbor, someone we know, is gay; they're not these predators." There's still that gap with trans people.

The problem is that when you ask people to come out, what is that gonna mean for people? Does it mean that they're gonna put their safety at risk? It's a burden for people, including myself. I know that every time I go up to speak, however many people are in the room now officially know a trans person. I'm likeable; I'm somebody they can connect to. It's a service for me to go out there in the world and put myself out there and say, "I'm a trans guy."

I have my own fears for safety for a very good reason. And so does my family. But I'm this white, educated, male lawyer. So I make my own choices around what privileges I have and what I want to do for the community.

How do you protect yourself?

DRU: It's severely stressful. You're pioneering wherever you go. You don't have support; you don't have proper mentorship. You have to trust your own gut. So it's a very difficult pioneering position to be in.

But on the flip side, I know that I have saved lives. *I literally change people's lives.* I've been doing LGBT activism for twenty years. I've been doing transgender-rights legal work for ten. And I literally know that I inspire people; there's a ripple effect. I think that's something to feel really good about.

Turning forty for me was realizing that you really need to prioritize yourself so that you can really be of more use to others in the world. I think that's not really taught. [M]y advice is that, as a trans person, taking care of yourself and staying alive is doing enough for the community. You don't owe anybody anything. Being alive would be really great. That is an act of self-care.

Dru expressed frustration that many major LGBTQ organizations have historically undermined trans concerns in favor of winning majority appeal with more "palatable" issues. And since marriage equality has been legalized in the United States, conservatives are looking for a new target in their war against the queer "agenda." The lack of education surrounding trans issues has left the community in a vulnerable position. The inevitable result, Dru concludes, is a law like HB-2.

Dru has been a role model for me as long as I've been in contact with him, which is a few years now. In addition to growing my understanding of trans rights, he showed me that trans people could have good lives, cool careers, and full relationships. He showed me you could have terrible ups and downs and still make it through.

What was your own coming-out like?

DRU: My first coming-out as gay was in my teens. And it was like, oh my gosh, it's not what my family was expecting; it goes against my religious upbringing, and everyone will be really disappointed with me, and I'm gonna face all kinds of hardships.

But there's, you know, community. There are gay bars. This

was before the Internet and pre-*Ellen*. I realized that there was some kind of positive.

The second coming-out, though, ten years later when I was twenty-seven, was very much the opposite of that. I didn't know any trans people. I didn't know of any community. I was extremely alone, and then I realized that, when I looked into it, I would have to cover all of any medical care I needed out-of-pocket, and the world thinks I'm crazy; there's literally a mental health diagnosis for this, and you're gonna be alone and probably kill yourself. It was a very dark time. I did not have any resources and can imagine that people have it way worse than I did, even now.

Do you have a relationship with your family today?

DRU: I do and it's amazing now. The very difficult years were when I first came out as gay. My family has a religious background, and it was a very big deal for them, not only for what they were expecting of me but also for everything that they knew and believed. It took them many years for their own process.

The times when you need your family the most are often the times when they're doing their own processing and having their own struggle and, therefore, the most unavailable. And that is just a horrible combination that I know a lot of people face. I absolutely faced that.

And my coming out as trans was obviously very challenging, but I think there was some groundwork laid from those pretty dark years of my first coming-out. So my family really messed up with pronouns for about a year, and my name was "old name— sorry!—new name." But it was really great because they were trying.

Dru explained he didn't enter law school intending to specialize in trans rights. "I think going to law school in part was a survival tactic because I felt so unsafe in the world," he reflected. "Being queer, being trans, you need all the tools you can to protect yourself."

He laughed as he recalled the e-mail he sent his extended family upon finishing his last year: "graduation & gender update."

We expanded on the idea of bad timing. I expressed that while being away from my family was terrible and *not* preferable, it was absolutely necessary for me while I was in college. I wouldn't have been able to maintain my emotional health otherwise; neither would my mother.

But while I had the resources of a decent insurance policy, a strong network of friends, and an LGBTQ-friendly college environment, many trans folk find themselves financially cut off, uninsured, un-housed, and floating.

DRU: Family acceptance is one of the keys to ending the suicide epidemic that we're seeing in the transgender community. And I think that families play a deeper role than people realize. What does that mean? We need to get families resources. We need to have visibility so that families have somewhere to turn to when somebody comes out.

That is such a critical and vulnerable time. We're losing people during that time period, and that is devastating not only to the movement but also to those families who couldn't turn that around, and figure that out, and be there in the way that the person might have needed them to be. I'm really glad that people survive that time period, but a lot of people don't. And I think that's really where we need to focus our energy.

I asked Dru what other avenues of support he used in his transition. He described therapy as being key, though he recalled that he "survived in *spite* of a bad therapist" who had no idea how to react to his coming-out.

Dru says he found a second therapist, one who claimed to be knowledgeable on gender issues, and worked with her for three years. He wasn't sure he wanted a medical transition, and for a time was very

against the idea. Eventually the time was right for him to start testosterone, but when he asked for a recommendation letter from his therapist,
she refused.

This "gatekeeping," a practice that controls or restricts access to
resources, was very traumatic for Dru. He tried again.

DRU: So then I found a different therapist a few months later, and
the first thing she said to me was, "You're in the driver's seat; I'm
in the back seat. And if you need a letter, you got it, but that's not
what this is about."

She took away the gatekeeping experience for me and said that
it was my decision, and she just wanted to support me. And that is
why I became who I am in the community, because I had that one
person who believed in me when I didn't have anybody else. I felt
empowered and supported.

He also credits an FTM (female-to-male) support group that his therapist pushed him to attend in adulthood. "I really didn't want to meet
any other trans people," he recalls. "I was terrified of all trans people
and all things trans. I really didn't want to be trans. And I forced myself
to go to one of these groups to have some peer support, and it was life
changing, because I realized that a lot of my experience was universal
and there was absolutely nothing wrong with me."

There's a remarkable cycle of support that people like Dru's therapist
set in motion. Support begets support. And now that Dru is helping
and advocating for people, the cycle continues.

**What would you say to younger trans people,
who are just figuring themselves out and figuring
things out, about protecting themselves?**

DRU: First of all, I'm so glad that you exist. I'm glad if you have
avoided any percentage of the damage that I experienced, just
as all the people who came before me helped me to avoid. I also

really know that it's still extremely challenging to be queer and/or trans in this world.

I just really want to do anything possible to keep people alive, keep people safe and happy and healthy. I think that leaning on each other and finding community and doing it better than the generation before is all key to that. I think there's gonna be things that you know about that I won't understand, and that you *do* have the answers to.

The one thing I always tell people at schools is [that] the bottom line is just trust yourself, because the world around you is telling you lots of different things, and you can't take that shit in.

ASK A TRANS PERSON: OSCAR

Oscar is a white, nonbinary transmasculine person who uses they/them/their *pronouns. Oscar grew up in Massachusetts and now attends college in Ohio.*

The following are select excerpts from our conversation, which covered Oscar's experiences as a nonbinary person, their coming-out, and changing notions of "self-care."

You may notice in my discussions with peers, we use words that may seem new or difficult to some readers. While context often illuminates meaning, you can always check back through the word banks between essays, where many of these words are simply defined.

If you were to explain to someone what gender is, how would you go about that?

OSCAR: I think pretty much anyone will probably agree that gender is very subjective to the culture in which it's defined. Masculinity is not as solidly defined as femininity. And that's because femininity is defined as what's lesser, and masculinity is defined as anything that's not lesser, which is supposed to be normal. Which is why privilege, in terms of gender at least, is so hard to acknowledge for many people who don't want to actively look at it.

The ways in which [gender] plays out, at least in our Euro-American culture [in the United States] is very different across racial lines. And I think that equating white feminism to black feminism, or even the experience of being a white woman to being a black woman, is entirely different. Whenever you talk about gender, you absolutely have to acknowledge race.

How would you describe "cisgender privilege"?

OSCAR: First of all it's important to define what "trans" is. And I have a little rant about this. I'm not trying to be exclusionary or anything, but "trans" heavily suggests moving in some direction. So that doesn't necessitate medical transitioning, but it does mean social transitioning, or the need to, or the compulsion to. And so I think a lot of people use "trans" as an umbrella term to include all nonbinary people as well. And we can be trans *and* nonbinary. But just because you are nonbinary does *not* make you trans.

I'm going to break that down a little.

Nonbinary people are exactly that: they identify outside or apart from the gender binary of men and women.

Oscar is trans because they moved away from their "starting place," their gender assignment at birth, and they are nonbinary because they don't strictly relate to the male or female gender. Furthermore, when Oscar uses the term "transmasculine," they are referring to a tendency toward identifying more along the masculine spectrum.

For context, I am also trans and I *do* identify within the binary. I identify as male, and use the pronouns we stereotypically associate with men, *he/him/his*.

Oscar's analysis of the nonbinary is important because it showcases the variety in people we often lump together as the "trans community."

"Cis-privilege," as Oscar explained, is not feeling the need to socially, medically, or otherwise move away from your starting point, your assigned gender.

OSCAR: So like one of the visceral ways that I feel my lack of cis privilege is in the medical industry. It's set up to entirely profit off of people who have illnesses both mental and physical and also disabilities. And it also is set up not only to profit off of but also to silence trans people. And not just silence but exclude trans people.

And I think "privilege" is such a sticky word because often people will be like, "Cis privilege is not having to transition," but there's nothing inherently privileged about *not* having to take hormones, you know? There's nothing inherently marginalized about *having* to take hormones. The issue comes when you look at who's *allowed* to get those hormones, who's able to get those hormones, and who has the resources. So the medical industry is one very strong aspect of cis privilege.

Also, cis privilege is not having to prove your gender.

This line of thought segued into our next subject: the objectification and hypersexualization of trans bodies. Earlier in this book I discussed the grossness of the moment when someone learns I'm trans. Oftentimes people give me a once-over, as if they are looking for the zipper.

Oscar admitted that for their first half-year on testosterone, they only told close friends and family. "Because," they explained, "I knew that the second I told people publicly, the first thing they would think about was my genitals."

Oscar is indeed the same Oscar mentioned earlier in connection with my surgery recovery. They are my second cousin through my stepfather. We played together during the summer as kids and later reconnected as trans adults. The experience of having a family member who is also trans has added so much to my life, and I'm incredibly grateful.

In addition to doting on their pet rats and cultivating plants, Oscar is also a gender advocate and student of queer studies. At the time of our speaking, they were entering the finals period of freshman year and had also just lost "Z.," a close trans friend, to suicide.

> OSCAR: No cis person I know wants to sit down and have this conversation with me, you know, because it doesn't affect their life; at least they don't *think* it does. But really it informs entirely how they affect other people's lives. Because we're so individualized in our culture, nobody cares deeply about how we affect the lives of other people. Well, not *nobody*, but so many people. We're conditioned not to.

Oscar commented that many *trans* people are also not interested in these kinds of discussions or in examining or challenging their own gendered experiences within a larger context. For years, I myself wasn't interested. I resented having the burden of proof placed on me *because* I was trans.

"And, it's like, that's fine," they explained regarding such attitudes. "It's *fine* that you're uncomfortable about this. *Cis* privilege is not having to think about these things. I get it."

At the same time, Oscar expressed that we have an obligation to tackle these issues. "It's not about being 'right,'" they emphasized. "It's about constantly growing and questioning."

What was your coming-out like?

> OSCAR: I think that oftentimes when people ask that question, what they're looking for is one story that entirely defines what "coming-out" is for that person. But it was a process that is comprised of many different experiences.
>
> My initial thought when someone asks me that, the story that I pull out of my ass or whatever, is when I definitively came out to my parents. But even that wasn't the beginning of it, because I had told them I think three or four times before that. And every time they had shut me down and thought they had taken care of

the problem. Each time it got harder, and each time I had to rev myself up for it and be like, "Okay, I'm ready to do it for real this time." And then I would back out.

And then I realized at one point, this is a matter of life or death. I absolutely cannot live like this anymore. And I have done it for years. At that point it was giving up, really, and acknowledging there are visceral and literal truths that are apparent in my body and my experience with it that are not there for everyone, and that I'm going to have to accept [those truths].

Oscar expressed that it didn't really occur to them that, as lesbians, their parents would react negatively to having a trans child.

OSCAR: That day I sat them down and I rationalized it as "Okay, I have two moms. They have met trans people before."

I had this really optimistic view of the LGBT community. I thought we were all in it together because I thought it should be obvious that we're all in it together, because so many of our identities are not mutually exclusive.

And so I told my parents, and they got really mad. And they thought that it was my way of separating myself from my femininity, and as second-wave lesbian feminists, they were very much connected to their womanhood. And they thought that it was me hating myself and me hating them; they thought they fucked up; they thought I was fucking up. They wanted to protect me from my own identity.

And where they were coming from was a well-meaning, but really damaging, misperception of what it means to be trans but also what it means to be a woman.

Oscar established their immediate needs as being called their new name and referred to with *they/them/theirs* pronouns. They also told their parents "that at some point I would need to go on hormones. And at some point I would need to legally change my name. And at some point I may need surgery, but that's in the future."

One of Oscar's moms, "A.," immediately expressed that she did not feel comfortable sharing a house with them. Their other mom, "B.," wanted to know that, if *some* trans people don't medically transition, why did Oscar have to?

Oscar was deeply hurt by B.'s question. They felt B. was inappropriately using the experiences of other trans people to invalidate the experiences, thoughts, and feelings Oscar was trying hard to convey.

Later, Oscar related the stress of this coming-out situation to the LGBTQ student group at their school, only to be shut down by their peers and the group's advisor. These people, who knew Oscar's family, dismissed their story on the grounds that it didn't seem characteristic of Oscar's liberal, queer parents.

> OSCAR: And I was like, "Okay, well you've successfully shut me up." And then I don't think I ever went back to [the LGBTQ group].
>
> That's another example of how cis non-straight people just really don't like trans people. They *really* don't like us. And it blows my mind every time I'm reminded. But they just *don't.*

Oscar's relationship with their parents has evolved and improved significantly over the years. Their family put me up during my hysto recovery and now takes a more active role in Oscar's trans experience.

> OSCAR: So there is this really cute quote I read a while ago, and it was like this parent thing, like "I was very homophobic, so God gave me three gay kids." And then there was some quote about "My kids are gay, and my church didn't accept them, so we found another church." And I think that religion can be used as a meta- phor for all the very fundamental frameworks that people use to look at their lives and understand the world around them.
>
> And I think that you *have* to be able to adapt your frame- works to fit the world instead of trying to fit the world into your framework.
>
> I was scared, I was very worried, I was very lonely, I felt like a

stranger in my own house. I was uncomfortable talking or looking at [my parents] for a while. But, like, I knew at the end of the
day—you know, maybe I have to wait ten years—but I know at
some point they will accept me. It is going to be a process.

Coming out doesn't necessarily begin and end with family. Once at college, Oscar struggled to get the administration to put their correct name
on the e-mail and attendance lists. And every time they interview for a
job, gender is salient.

Oscar summarized: "My entire life is coming out to people. Or, I
will be coming out to people for my entire life. Coming out is a very
lived reality for me."

**What are sources of support for you, and what
are ways that you take care of yourself specifically?**

OSCAR: If I had to pick one thing that is the most damaging
aspect of our culture across the board—and how it plays into
capitalism and different marginalizations—it's how individual-
ized we are. We are not allowed to be vulnerable. It's not even that
we're not *allowed* to; we cannot *want* to be vulnerable. We are not
supposed to be okay with being vulnerable.

And part of that has a lot to do with gender, and vulnerability
and emotion are seen as feminine traits and thus devalued. And I
don't know which came first, the chicken or the egg, so to speak,
but I know that these two things are inherently linked, and this
thing is inherently gendered. And I think that learning to overcome that is incredibly crucial to survival.

I know Z. [Oscar's trans friend who committed suicide]
could not tell people things. She was not very open. But even then
there's a difference between not being open and not being able to
reach out. And she was both. And the only way that I know I can
be happy is if I surround myself with people who love and care
about me. And not just that, but if I am also someone who loves
and cares about other people.

So I think that something that is so crucial to survival is interconnectedness and community. And I know in Massachusetts I worked very, very hard. Because I never found a friend group at school, I was forced to look for friends in other places. And because of that, and because I'm pretty decent at social skills to say the least, I worked very hard to—and was able to build—a network of people who cared about me.

Here [in college] I've done the same thing. I have fucking friends all over campus, and I'm very loved, and even that sometimes isn't enough. Because Z. was very, very loved. She was a fucking campus celebrity. And so there are internal components to that. But for me that is one of the most important things for healing and growth.

I think one thing that is easy to get caught up in is this idea that healing means you're happy. And that being fulfilled means happy. But those are entirely not the same thing.

So I started thinking of my life in terms of fulfillment. And so that's when I . . . really dedicated myself to doing work that I was proud of, and not just work in organizations but also work like interpersonally, like caring for my friends, caring for myself. I started getting plants around then. I started growing plants. I have rats now. There are things that fulfill me but do not make me "happy."

So, yeah. That's how I take care of myself.

ASK A TRANS PERSON: ALYSSANDRA

Alyssandra "Aly" Taylor is a trans woman who sometimes identifies as a trans feminine nonbinary person. She uses she/her/hers *and* they/them/theirs *pronouns.*

Aly is an actress and artist who aims to further trans visibility and create more opportunities for queer people to tell their stories. At the time of our speaking, she had just wrapped Charm *at Minneapolis's Mixed Blood Theatre and moved back to Boston to prepare for Company One's summer 2016 production of* T Party.

The following are select excerpts from our conversation, which engaged the life-saving effects of representation and Aly's commitment to a conception of "trans" that is not defined by medical procedures.

How did you get interested in performing and acting? And why do you think theater is a good medium for advocacy?

ALY: When I was in eighth grade I discovered that I really liked to read out loud in class. And people liked me to read out loud in class because I would give people different voices and make it kinda funny or really dramatic. And when I got to high school I was in drama club, and in tenth grade I was the lead male role. I really just liked acting and being able to connect with an audience and tell a story and have them "vibe."

If an actor is good you should be able to connect to their story, and connect with their emotions and how real the character is. If you put your all into a character, people will feel that, whether it's onstage or onscreen. And that's what I want to do.

Aly joined the True Colors troupe in Boston, a theater program that engages and trains LGBTQ youth as artists and leaders. They write and put on plays based on their lives, stories that no one else is telling. Aly credits her time with True Colors as solidifying her passion for writing and acting.

For her, art and activism are a natural combination. Not only can theater and film depict a variety of human perspectives, but they also can provide role models or, in Laverne Cox's words, "possibility models." In Cordelia Fine's 2010 book *Delusions of Gender,* she contends, "People's self-evaluations, aspirations, and performance are all enhanced by encountering the success of similar role models—and the more similar, the better."

ALY: I realize how important it is to see yourself, and to imagine yourself in any role, any position, anything you want to do in life.

As her own possibility models, Aly brought up prime-time TV actresses who are also black women: Angela Bassett (*American Horror Story*), Viola Davis (*How to Get Away with Murder*), Kerry Washington (*Scandal*), and prolific writer and TV showrunner Shonda Rhimes. Aly pointed out that many actors of color spend years in smaller parts and have a far more limited number of big-break opportunities than white people.

Media representation *is* shifting to include a more diverse (real) spread of human beings, yet our screens and stages are still dominated by white actors, particularly white male actors. If you just look at box-office statistics, you get a strong picture of the current gender disparity.

The Center for the Study of Women in Television and Film's survey of the top one hundred films of 2015 found that women accounted for 34 percent of major characters; only 13 percent of those were black, with Latina and Asian women coming in at 4 percent and 3 percent, respectively.

Another survey of women's involvement behind the scenes was even more dire, finding that, in 2015, women made up 19 percent of "all directors, writers, producers, executive producers, editors, and cinematographers working on the top 250 domestic grossing films." The second study doesn't even factor in race, and neither includes queer identities. And as Aly herself proves, lack of talent isn't the issue; opportunity is.

ALY: Laverne Cox won an award for being on *Orange Is the New Black*, but she's barely on that show. I like the fact that she's gonna be Dr. Frank-N-Furter [in the *Rocky Horror Picture Show* reboot], and the fact that she'll be on the CBS show *Doubt*. Amiyah [Scott, a trans actress and model] got cast on *Star*, which is gonna be on Fox in January.

That trans actresses are getting roles is important—Alexandra

Billings is gonna be on *Transparent*—but I want to create more roles for people of color. Especially trans kids.

Anyone who's on that spectrum, whether they're trans, genderqueer, gender nonconforming, agender, bigender, there's still not a lot of visibility. There's not a lot of roles out there. And if they're not gonna give them to us, we just have to create them.

How do you look at gender and how do you define "trans"?

ALY: I think gender is a spectrum. I don't believe in it just being two genders, but I think some people really adhere to being one gender or the other. I don't think that's a problem. I think that's fine. But I also believe people exist within that, and we have to make space for the people who live in between.

For me, personally, trans is being assigned a gender/sex at birth and not feeling completely comfortable with that label.

I think the important thing to remember about being trans is *you don't actually have to transition*. Like that's never a thing. It's just not being completely comfortable with the gender identity and/or sex assigned at birth.

What was your coming-out like?

ALY: It was very stressful. I feel like a lot of my friends and people outside of my family [and] some of my relatives supported me, and then a lot of people in my family were not okay with it. Some people were.

[When] I finally did say, "I'm transitioning; I'm doing this," I was nineteen, and I got kicked out. And it was my senior year of high school, and I was getting accepted to colleges and starting hormones and sleeping on my aunt's couch and living with [one of my sisters] and trying to work to support myself. That was stressful, and I actually stopped talking to my mom for a long time. We got into a lot of arguments that were mostly about me being trans and me feeling disrespected. And I was definitely disrespectful in return, something that I'm not completely proud of. But I think I was just trying to survive.

My coming-out—it was a mixed bag. But overall I don't think it was the worst coming-out, and I'm glad that I had support.

Aly lived with her sisters and an aunt for periods of time. "I didn't know where I was going a lot of times in college when we would be on breaks," she explained. "I would be figuring that shit out a few days before I would have to."

I asked how her relationship with her family has progressed. She said it varies. While two of her brothers see her as their sister and have even gotten a little too "overprotective," Aly and another of her brothers don't talk at all.

ALY: My sisters are still very supportive. I don't know; I don't really talk to my dad, but he does tell me that he loves me and wishes me a happy birthday and [isn't] disrespectful. So, like, you know, that's good. And my mother and I are working on things.

She hasn't come around to calling me "she," but I think I've gotten her to stop calling me "he," so that's good.

Whether it was other family members or friends, or school or organizations, what was the most helpful support network for you?

ALY: All of that. All of that was needed to help me survive. I don't think I would have gotten through [my coming-out] because I was so trapped in my head a lot of the time and angry and sad when I first transitioned. Happy for me but also angry that I was losing so much and for such a dumb reason.

Aly cited Boston's Alliance of Gay, Lesbian, Bisexual, and Transgender Youth (BAGLY) and the city's renowned LGBTQ wellness center,

Fenway Health, as havens. She counted GLAAD, trans-positive doctors, and her friends and their families, as well as her aunts, sisters, and cousins as necessary support. She also joined a performance collective at her college, a group called "Flawless Brown," which aims to tell the stories of women of color. Whether it was knowing she had to get up for rehearsal or having a validating exchange with another queer student, Aly found seemingly small measures of community added up to great effect.

In one instance during her freshman year, Aly showed up to her assigned dorm room to find the wrong nametag on the door. She told her RA and he had it changed in a matter of hours.

**What would you say to someone younger
who's trans and dealing with these questions,
the anger, the sadness, for the first time?**

ALY: The first thing is, remember that you're not alone. You are not the only person dealing with this. Things do actually get better. Sometimes they get worse—a lot worse—before they get better.

Something else to keep in mind is when people get your pronouns wrong and you're younger and you're in that angry-sensitive mode when you start to transition, lots of people aren't doing it on purpose. Sometimes people slip up. Allow for that, just because it will be easier on you and your anger, and it will be easier on your relationships with people.

A lot of times you don't think people are trying, but they are. Make space for them.

But also keep in mind that *you* know who you are, and even if who you are changes, that's okay because we *make* who we are. You kind of "find" yourself, but for the most part you *make* yourself. Be who you wanna be and don't let anyone else tell you differently, even if you hear a bunch of people calling you a boy and you know you're a girl. Keep that. You keep that. Hold onto that and don't let anyone take that from you.

And also if you're okay with your body, don't let any other

trans person tell you that you need to do work or be on hormones or any of that. None of that makes you trans. If you know in your heart and your mind that you are who you are, don't let anyone change that; don't let anybody push you into anything you don't want to do.

Aly then mentioned that she didn't endorse the word "passing." As discussed in other sections, "passing" refers to the ability of a trans person to assimilate into the binary, to be undetectable as trans.

Can you elaborate a little bit about why the term "passing" can be damaging?

ALY: Because it implies that, one, if you "pass," that you're lying about something or you're "getting one over." I hate that. And it also implies that women and men are only supposed to look one sort of way.

You shouldn't have to look a certain way to be regarded by the pronouns you want to use or have people look at you and respect you for who you are.

"Passing" is a complex issue that is often very personal for trans folk. It is also the basis for many gender compliments, such as "You look great; no one would ever know you were trans!"

While statements like this can seem like a real self-esteem boost, they're also creepy and invasive. An outsider is evaluating your body and literally judging if you "pass" the test of looking. And while many trans people "pass" both with and without medical intervention, there are those who *don't* and *won't* ever blend in. As Aly argued, "passing" also demands adherence to strict cultural beauty standards for men and women, standards that are impossible for *anyone* to meet.

What is self-care for you?

ALY: Definitely being onstage. I have to act. I have to either be acting or creating. I need to be working on my art, because that is my self-care.

Also, taking time away from social media or from the news and watching sometimes mindless television, or just reading a book, something that's not so depressing. I can't handle all the news about black people being killed or trans women and trans men constantly being attacked or harassed. I just can't. I can't handle that. Being woke is a lot for me.

But, also, treat youself. You know? Like, do what you wanna do. Have fun, go out with friends, spend time alone if you need to, listen to music, write.

Aly listed therapy as another important means of support. As a survivor of sexual abuse and a trans person, she says it can be incredibly helpful to vent "to somebody who isn't going to judge you and who you know isn't going to tell anybody."

ALY: It's important to just be able to be like "ugh!" and talk about all the shit that's bothering you, and get it off your chest so it's not trapped up inside of you. Don't let that anger and that sadness just sit in you and take over.

ASK A TRANS PERSON: MAL

Mal M. is a genderqueer transmasculine person who uses they/them/ their pronouns. They grew up in the Midwest and now work as a broad- cast journalist in Minnesota. Over the years, Mal has volunteered for many LGBTQ organizations, coordinating educational outreach, public events, and support groups. At the time of our interview, they lived in San Francisco and worked for a marketing company.

The following are select excerpts from our conversation, which covered Mal's experiences working in such organizations, their journey to selfhood, and their relationship to the various expectations associated with transitioning.

How has your understanding of your gender,
and your gender identity, changed in the last few years?

MAL: So I first heard of "trans" in high school. I don't think
it was really anything I ever contemplated. I came out as
bisexual in middle school, which would have been like ten
years ago.

Mal expressed that they never really knew of many other LGBTQ
people in their Midwestern hometown. Coming out openly in middle
school, as they did, was not the norm. Then, in high school, Mal came
out as a lesbian.

MAL: But it wasn't until my senior year that things about gender
got complicated.

I think I started just *contemplating* transitioning. And heard
more about it. And saw a lot of masculine traits within myself that
I wanted more [of] through transitioning. I cut my hair short; I
started just wearing men's clothes. I think this was very hard on
my parents, and it was hard on me too because, you know, you
want support from your parents and your family more than you
want acceptance from others.

Even going back to elementary school, I was always such a
"tomboy." I played on the boys' baseball team for years. And, so,
I think a lot of people understood, even before I did, why I was
having such "masculine" tendencies.

And I think my parents didn't want to see this, and other
people who were close to me didn't want to see this, didn't want
to accept it.

When I came to college I had a female roommate. It felt
like I was being shoved back in the closet again. And I didn't
know if I was ready to fully come out, if I was ready to fully transition yet.

And so then I started coming out in select places. I joined an
outside LGBT group besides just the one at my college, so I could

try out a new name and stuff like that. And it felt affirming, so I decided to come out in between my freshman and sophomore year as trans male.

As Mal entered college, anxiety surrounding their transition grew. They didn't feel comfortable speaking to family about it, and meanwhile, their body dissatisfaction intensified. Mal edited their broadcast journalism footage with dismay, dreading watching and listening to themselves.

MAL: I was very depressed and suicidal in between my sophomore and junior year. So I decided to see a therapist to talk about it, to talk about transitioning. That winter, I started testosterone. And it was great; I was excited about it.

But through my transition, things like voice changes and stuff, that *also* became overwhelming. And so I started to think deeper about how I fit in with other people around me. And for a long time I was on the wrong dose of T, so I kind of went through . . . not transition but not reversal. I actually went through like menopause for a few months.

Their doctor, a practitioner within a major medical organization that championed LGBTQ health care, did not make it clear to Mal how often they were supposed take the hormone dose. It was supposed to be every week; Mal took it every other week. If that sounds odd to readers, understand that many endocrinologists prescribe biweekly doses.

Essentially, Mal's body didn't have enough testosterone to take over as the dominant hormone but still had enough to interfere with estrogen production. For someone experiencing gender dissonance, the dose mix-up was anything but harmless. Mal called it the worst time of their life.

MAL: I felt really sick. It was horrible. So the anxiety of that forced me to think more deeply about gender and what I wanted from transitioning. I definitely had this moment where I was like,

"I need to just stop. I don't know if I want to move forward. I don't know if I really necessarily want to move backward. I think I just need to take this time to reassess all these things that I thought I knew about myself."

And that was a huge journey to go on. I kind of took time to reassess. At first I told all my friends, "I think I want to de-transition." But then I was like, "No, that's stupid. I don't want to de-transition. I don't want to be going back to female. And I don't know if I necessarily want to keep moving forward as just male identified. I think I'm just *me*. I think I'm just Mal. I think I need to just move forward, just as myself."

I think that's just how I've kind of approached gender since. That's why I use *they/them/theirs*. Just because I still don't see myself as necessarily female or male. I think I definitely am more towards the more male or masculine side. But I don't think I see myself as necessarily male.

Do you feel there is a pressure to transition medically and to "pass"?

MAL: Yeah. I think there [are] three main components to why people medically transition. One, what you want for yourself. Two, what others want for you, aka society. And three, I think there's also pressure from the trans community.

I hated my body, I hated myself, I hated my voice, I hated my hairline. I hated that when I put on men's clothing that it always fit wrong. There was a lot of pressure that I put on myself, of just all these different things that I was not.

And I thought that by medically transitioning, I could fit better into men's clothing, that I could like my body more. So there was a lot of pressure that I put on myself.

And then I think, while support groups really helped me, a lot of the people that surrounded me were very binary identified. I didn't know a lot of genderqueer people. So I think that also put pressure on me.

The phrase *binary identified*, as used above, refers to trans folk like myself who identify within the binary of male/female, men/women.

Trans people who "pass" or fit more seamlessly within this binary, are able to exercise their rights with a degree of safety and comfort other trans and gender-variant people do not have. The idea of "passing" as a goal or way of validating gender is further discussed and critiqued in Alyssandra's interview.

Mal repeatedly acknowledged a severe pressure to meet *other people's* expectations of a transition. Even when Mal looked to other trans peers for support, having binary images reflected back only reinforced the aim of looking "like that."

They explained that by creating a trans-life narrative, wherein someone has to have surgery and "pass," we are just creating another unfair standard, another gender box. This goes back to Mal's assertion that cis people are always looking to hear the same familiar "coming out" story, to be assured, for example, that a person has *always* felt like a boy since birth.

MAL: The truth is that I have *not* always felt this way. And I think for a long time I had to be firm in saying that, even though I didn't necessarily feel that way. I have definitely always felt different than my peers, but I don't think that's necessarily because I'm trans. I think it has to do with a lot of different factors with my identity: of being Hispanic, of being queer identified, of just not falling into norms within my community.

I think once you're able to realize you can go on your own path and go on your own journey, it's extremely liberating.

As a student, you were involved in many LGBTQ groups and organizations. What were some of the institutional problems you ran up against?

MAL: I think that when you think you're on the top, that there's no way to go further. And that's the biggest problem that I see even with LGBT groups, with colleges that get ranked among the top for LGBT issues, with cities that are known as queer utopias. And I think when it comes down to it, they're really not. They themselves have a lot of work to continue to press on with.

**You expressed how much stress and anxiety
you had around speaking to your family about gender.
What is your relationship to your family like now?**

MAL: So, I haven't formally come out to my family, though I know that they know that I was on testosterone. I found out through my sister that my dad had asked her about it, because I guess it came up on my insurance bill. So I know it's out there, and I know that at any time they could ask me. But I think that they're just waiting at this point for me to talk about it. And even though I've come to terms with myself being trans for the last six years or more, it's still something that I'm not ready to talk about.

Mal worries about being unable to meet their family's "expectations of a transition," that their parents will have too many questions. They worry their family won't understand their gender identity or be able to envision a healthy relationship with a genderqueer child.

MAL: I think that's why I've held off. My sister knows. But even as a lesbian, she hasn't always been perfect, I would say. When I did first come out to her, when I first came out my senior year of high school, she didn't understand and she just wasn't ready for that. And I, looking back, don't blame her.

And now she's great. She's more educated about trans issues, about trans identities, and through college has met other gender-queer and agender and gender-nonconforming people. I think that, over time, she realized she needed to "read up" on this.

My friends in college were great, and I think that's why I've been so open and honest with them through everything, because they said, "I don't know, but that's okay because you're my friend, and I don't care what I call you or how you look as long as, at the end of the day, we can still watch scary movies together and do crazy shenanigans."

I think that my family, when I was first coming out and first started wearing men's clothing and stuff like that, they didn't show me immediate unconditional love. And that was the hardest part. So I've still just been reserved because of those moments that I needed my family and they weren't there exactly how I needed them to be. So I think that's why I've been holding out, waiting for a perfect moment. There have been moments that I certainly could have said something and chose not to, and I regret those.

How do you take care of yourself?

MAL: I never really had that great of friends in high school, so having *amazing* friends in college was my self-care. I had different groups, like my best friends that I could go to when I just needed to get out of my head and play video games or go outside. And then I also had a great support group through the LGBT groups that I was involved in. I was able to connect with other people to feel a deeper sense of community.

Now that I'm out of college, I'm struggling to find a community. Especially in San Francisco, where it feels very gay-male heavy, and I'm not a gay male. I think it's hard for me to find a community. I don't necessarily want a group of just *trans* friends; I want a group of different LGBT identities, and I haven't quite found that yet.

And I think I just keep searching for others who have a similar identity to me. Or to have some divine sign of what I should do for my transition, but so far it hasn't come, so I think I'm still looking out for it.

But in the meantime, my self-care is just surrounding myself with my friends and my partner and people who deeply care about me.

Donald's Reading List

For those interested in learning more about trans lives and gender-variant perspectives—or if you're simply down to hang out with a rad book—this is a good place to start!

The lists below provide a framework for understanding trans and gender non-conforming people throughout history, and how they have been represented (or not). Some of these books revolve around transness, some merely include trans characters, and others explore the changing position of gender in American society. Some are written by trans people; many are not. Although there are several exceptions, titles here deal mostly with Western perspectives on trans identity.

I compiled these books (and one journal) based on my own reading, outside recommendations, and research. It's not comprehensive, but within these categories, I intended to include some of the most seminal trans works, as well as the works of newer authors. There are also workbooks designed to give families a head start on trans issues, and offer parenting guidance.

Please note that topics tackled by writers, especially in the memoir genre, can be significantly difficult and graphic, with depictions of drug use, sexual abuse, and physical violence.

Fiction

Annabel, by Kathleen Winter
Breakfast on Pluto, by Patrick McCabe
The Collection: Short Fiction from the Transgender Vanguard,
    edited by Riley MacLeod and Ryka Aoki
Kafka on the Shore, by Haruki Murakami
Kitchen, by Banana Yoshimoto
Myra Breckinridge, by Gore Vidal
Orlando, by Virginia Woolf
Stone Butch Blues, by Leslie Feinberg
The Well of Loneliness, by Radclyffe Hall

Young Adult Fiction

Almost Perfect, by Brian Katcher
Being Emily, by Rachel Gold
A Boy Like Me, by Jennie Wood
George, by Alex Gino
If I Was Your Girl, by Meredith Russo
Luna, by Julie Anne Peters
Parrotfish, by Ellen Wittlinger
Symptoms of Being Human, by Jeff Garvin

General Interest Nonfiction

*Delusions of Gender: How Our Minds, Society, and Neurosexism
    Create Difference,* by Cordelia Fine
Far from the Tree: Parents, Children, and the Search for Identity,
    by Andrew Solomon
Out of the Past: Gay and Lesbian History from 1869 to the Present,
    by Neil Miller
Sex Changes: Transgender Politics, by Patrick Califia
Transgender History, by Susan Stryker

Transgender Studies Quarterly (journal), edited by Paisley Currah
   and Susan Stryker
*Whipping Girl: A Transsexual Woman on Sexism and the Scape-
   goating of Femininity*, by Julia Serano

Family & Community

Artistic Expressions of Transgender Youth, by Tony Ferraiolo
Beyond Magenta: Transgender Teens Speak Out, by Susan Kuklin
*The Gender Creative Child: Pathways for Nurturing and
   Supporting Children Who Live Outside Gender Boxes*,
   by Diane Ehrensaft
*The Gender Quest Workbook: A Guide for Teens and Young Adults
   Exploring Gender Identity*, by Deborah Coolhart, Rylan J. Tesla,
   and Jayme Peta
*Trans Bodies, Trans Selves: A Resource for the Transgender Commu-
   nity*, by Laura Erickson-Schroth
The Transgender Child: A Handbook for Families and Professionals,
   by Stephanie A. Brill and Rachel Pepper
Transgender 101: A Simple Guide to a Complex Issue, by Nicholas
   Teich

Memoir & Nonfiction Anthologies

Becoming a Visible Man, by Jamison Green
Being, by Zach Ellis
Gender Failure, by Rae Spoon and Ivan E. Coyote
Gender Outlaws: The Next Generation, by Kate Bornstein and
   S. Bear Bergman
*Man Alive: A True Story of Violence, Forgiveness, and Becoming
   a Man*, by Thomas Page McBee
Nobody Passes: Rejecting the Rules of Gender and Conformity,
   edited by Mattilda Bernstein Sycamore
Queer & Trans Artists of Color: Stories of Some of Our Lives,
   interviews by Nia King

Redefining Realness: My Path to Womanhood, Identity, Love
   & So Much More, by Janet Mock
She's Not There: A Life in Two Genders, by Jennifer Finney Boylan
Trans/Portraits: Voices from Transgender Communities, by Jackson
   Wright Shultz
Trauma Queen: A Memoir, by Lovemme Corazón

Acknowledgments

MARY COLLINS: First and foremost I want to thank my remarkable son, Donald Collins, for having the courage and open-mindedness to engage in this book project with me.

I would also like to thank my mother, Constance Collins, who showed Donald and me the road back to each other; my siblings, James Collins, Elizabeth Collins, and Tricia Collins, for never walking away from what must have been a fraught situation for the extended family.

In general, I had few people to turn to whom I could trust to listen to my fears and questions without judgment during Donald's high school and college years, but those who did step up for me provided much-needed solace during the hardest hours. Thank you, Susan McElhinney, Tom Vasko, Sal Lilienthal, Michael Sloan, Scott Franklin, Russell Gardner, and Linda Wagner.

Many of the parents of transgender teens and college-age students who I contacted for this book shared my wariness and lack of trust in counselors and health professionals, which made my conversations with Libby McKnight and Elijah Nealy, two professionals who helped me find parents for my Story Exchange section, especially affirming. They understood immediately what *At the Broken Places* could offer families and worked hard to convince parents to trust me with their stories.

Of course, I must also thank the parents who spoke to me, either anonymously or on the record, including those who did not want me to publish their stories but still shared their experiences with me. We all felt comforted by talking about our shared challenges.

This project started as an essay that I wrote for a summer Yale Writer's Workshop directed by Eileen Pollack, director of the MFA program at the University of Michigan at the time. I want to thank her for giving Donald and me an enthusiastic introduction to Beacon Press when we were ready to shop our proposal. I also did a book-manuscript exchange with my dear friend Paula Whitacre—she edited our project, and I provided feedback on her fine biography of Civil War heroine Julia Wilbur, who helped escaped slaves build a new life in Virginia. Few things in life have given me as much pleasure as being a part of the community of letters in the United States, and Eileen and Paula represent just two of the many fine writers, editors, and other professionals I've worked with over my career.

From the moment Beacon Press accepted *At the Broken Places*, I knew we had found the best possible home for our book. The staff embraced our work with such enthusiasm and professionalism at every part of the process, from the fine copyedit by managing editor Susan Lumenello to the hard work on the cover design by Louis Roe. They even met with us in person for more than two hours in Boston, a level of engagement that's hard to find in publishing anymore.

I wish to close with a special thanks to Michael Bronski, who graciously agreed to include *At the Broken Places* in his series, Queer Action/Queer Ideas, and to Beacon's editorial director, Gayatri Patnaik, who embraced our project with such verve from the moment she saw our proposal. To receive such a welcome from such an experienced editor on such an emotionally complex project validated for me that Donald and I had indeed reflected carefully and with humanity on our journey and used our shared love of writing and books to create something we can both be proud of.

DONALD COLLINS: The kindest people in life never expect anything in return, and indeed I will never be able to return the kindness extended to me by the people named here.

First off, thanks to my mother for her capacity to weather total honesty throughout the duration of this collaboration. I love you and am so happy to have painful honesty over silence, denial, and estrangement. I am forever in awe at all you accomplished as a working single parent.

Thank you to my grandmother Constance, whose name suggests the exact unfailing love and devotion she provided my mother and me. Thank you, Aunt Tricia, Aunt Betty, and Uncle Jimmy.

Thank you to my dad, Andrew, for his continued support. I already had one father walk away—I hope you know that you are loved and appreciated.

I'd like to thank the Loomis Chaffee School for its conscientious efforts to create a safe environment for LGBTQ students, and I extend total gratitude to all the individuals and educators there who made my experience so worthwhile: Andrew Watson, Andrea Rooks, Mark Zunino, Jennifer McCandless, Dennis Robbins, Deb and Frank Aniello, and Robin Willard, among others. Thank you, Sus, Joanna, Shondaray, Susannah, Garrett, Fred, Dru, Xandee, and Palmer Dormitory.

Shout out to Emerson College for providing me with a creative and interdisciplinary undergrad experience, and to the educators and administrators there committed to helping queer students and spreading gender education. Thank you, Tulasi Srinivas, for opening my mind and helping me see a world beyond myself. Thank you, Jane Powers, for all your medical guidance and personal encouragement. Thank you to my LB and Colonial RA staffs. Thank you, Brittany Burke, Katie Krause, and Scott Wallace.

To my health-care professionals, Dr. Trantham, Dr. Honen, Dr. Hulinsky, Dr. Johnson, and Dr. Travias: *Thank you all for being so good.*

Thank you to the Phi Alpha Tau fraternity and the spring 2013 pledge class for its unconditional support and community. I'm particularly grateful for the care of Christian Bergren-Aragon, Brendan Scully, Daniel Irwin, Ryan Sweeney, Christopher Kavanah, Chris Largent, Eric Maxwell, Benjamin Lindsay, Nic Damasio, Mari Watson, Alicia Carroll, John Lewis, Darian Carpenter, Ethan Weiser, Carey Shannon, and, of course, the incomparable Mike Dunbar.

To my friend Skylar Spear and his family: I love you all so much. I couldn't have made it to senior prom, never mind anywhere else, without you.

Additional thanks to Tony Ferraiolo and Dru Levasseur, for their live-saving work, and to Tonasia, Mal, Oscar, Alyssandra, Helena, Maha, Caroline, my wonderful roommate Christine, and my friends Kassie King and Matthew Begbie. Love you.

I'd also like to extend massive appreciation to Beacon Press for the care and respect they directed toward our project and for the contributions of Louis Roe and Perpetua Charles to this book's design and marketing.

Sources

Introductions
Word Bank

F. Scott Fitzgerald, *The Great Gatsby* (1925; New York: Scribner, 2004).

Annamarie Jagose, *Queer Theory: An Introduction* (New York: New York University Press, 1997).

Julia Serano, *Whipping Girl* (Berkeley, CA: Seal Press, 2007).

Susan Stryker, *Transgender History* (Berkeley, CA: Seal Press, 2008).

Pronouns and Body Parts
Who Wears the Pants?

Jon I. Einarsson and Yoko Suzuki, "Total Laparoscopic Hysterectomy: 10 Steps Toward a Successful Procedure," *Obstetrics & Gynecology* 2, no. 1 (Winter 2009): 57–64.

Jaime M. Grant, Lisa A. Mottet, Justin Tanis, Jack Harrison, Jody L. Herman, and Mara Keisling, *Injustice at Every Turn: A Report of the National Transgender Discrimination Survey* (Washington: National Center for Transgender Equality and National Gay and Lesbian Task Force, 2011).

Virginia Woolf, *Orlando* (1928; Boston: Mariner Books, 1973).

Mismatch

American Foundation for Suicide Prevention, which analyzed the results of the National Transgender Discrimination Survey, 2015. *On the more than 40 percent (41 percent) of transgender children who attempt suicide.*

Peter Beinart, "Why America Is Moving Left," *Atlantic,* January/February 2016. *For the YouGov survey on those who feel that being transgender is morally wrong.*

Anthony Faiola, "Europe Pushes for Gender-Neutral World," *Washington Post,* June 18, 2015.

Anemona Hartocollis, "New Girl in School: Transgender Surgery at 18," *New York*

Times, June 17, 2015. *For information on Swedish studies and growing trend towards making gender switch at ever younger ages.*

Jamie Hawkesworth, photographer, "One," *New York Times Sunday Magazine,* October 16, 2014, 166.

Dr. Dean Hokanson, author interview, West Hartford, CT, spring 2015. *On the two-step process for male bodies and brains in womb.*

Ian Peate, "Understanding Key Issues in Gender-Variant Children and Young People," *British Journal of Nursing* 17 (September 25–October 8, 2008): 1114–18.

Steve Petrow, "Civilities," *Washington Post,* October 27, 2014.

Peg Rosen, "You Really Do Need Your Ovaries," *More Magazine,* June 2009. *She cites a study with thirty thousand participants conducted by the Nurses' Health Study.* William Parker from the John Wayne Cancer Center, Santa Monica, CA, "Long-Term Mortality Associated with Oophorectomy versus Ovarian Conservation in the Nurses' Health Study," *Obstetric Gynecology* 121, no. 4 (April 2013): 709–16.

Katherine Rosman, "Me, Myself and Mx," *New York Times,* June 5, 2015.

Julie Scelfo, "They," *New York Times,* special education section, February 8, 2015. *On the use of gender-neutral pronouns at the University of Vermont.*

Matthew Sturdevant, "More Insurers Cover Sex Changes," *Hartford Courant,* October 29, 2014.

US Food and Drug Administration, "Menopause and Hormones: Common Questions," http://www.fda.gov/ForConsumers/ByAudience/ForWomen/ucm 118624.htm. Last updated September 28, 2015. *For information on menopause and oophorectomy.*

Lewis Wolpert, "Are Girls and Boys Different?," *Telegraph,* September 14, 2014.

———, "Yes, It's Official, Men Are from Mars and Women Are from Venus and Here's the Science to Prove It," *Telegraph* (UK), October 31, 2014.

Endings and Beginnings
Mapping Modern Grief

John Archer, *The Nature of Grief: The Evolution and Psychology of Reactions to Loss* (New York: Routledge, 1999). *On separation anxiety and the evolution of grief.*

George Bonanno, *The Other Side of Sadness: What the New Science of Bereavement Tells Us About Life After Loss* (New York: Basic Books, 2009). *On how humans are hardwired to grieve, and on the positive side of grief.*

Mikaela Cowley, "Heartbreak Can Take a Physical Toll," Tribune Newspapers, March 6, 2013. *On data the heart sometimes enlarges when one is grieving or under great duress.*

"Calculating Migration Expectancy Using ACS Data," US Census Bureau, 2015, https://www.census.gov/hhes/migration/about/cal-mig-exp.html. *For data on how often the average American moves in his or her lifetime (11.7 times).*

National Survey of Families and Households, Intergenerational Proximity;

National Center for Family and Marriage Research. *For data showing that one family in five has a child who moves far from home.*

Paul Ekman, *Emotions Revealed: Recognizing Faces and Feelings to Improve Communication and Emotional Life* (New York: Times Books, 2003). *On the use of facial muscles to show grief and happiness.*

Ted Gup, "Diagnosis: Human," *New York Times*, April 3, 2013; Benedict Carey, "A Tense Compromise on Defining Disorders," *New York Times*, December 11, 2012; Stephen Adams, "Grief Should Not Be Treated Like Depression," *Daily Telegraph* (London), February 17, 2012. *On grief defined as a mental disorder.*

Janice L. Krupnick et al., "Bereavement During Childhood and Adolescence," in *Bereavement: Reactions, Consequences, and Care* (Washington, DC: National Academies Press, 1984), ed. Marian Osterweis and Frederic Solomon. *On data that only 4 percent of children under age fifteen lose a parent.*

Lancet, "Living with Grief," editorial, *Lancet* 379, no. 9816 (February 18, 2012): 589.

John Ratey and Eric Hagerman, *Spark: The Revolutionary New Science of Exercise and the Brain* (New York: Little, Brown, 2008). *On movement and improving depression.*

Jessica Samakow, "Gender Conformity Study Says Kids Outside of Norm Are at Increased Risk of Abuse," *Huffington Post*, February 21, 2012, article about a 2012 study in *Pediatrics* on data showing that 10 percent of children under age eleven identify outside gender "norms."

Birds of Spring

Stephanie A. Brill and Rachel Pepper, *The Transgender Child: A Handbook for Families and Professionals* (San Francisco: Cleis Press, 2008).

Laverne Cox, blog post, Lavernecox.tumblr.com, June 2, 2015.

Grant et al., *Injustice at Every Turn.*

Evelyn Waugh, *Brideshead Revisited* (1945; New York: Back Bay Books, 2012).

Sharing Our Story with Others
Word Bank

Arika Okrent, "What Is the Origin of the Phrase 'Coming Out of the Closet'?," *Mental Floss*, May 3, 2013, http://mentalfloss.com/article/50405/what-origin-phrase-come-out-closet.

Donald Has Something He Wants to Tell the Class

Judith Butler, *Gender Trouble: Feminism and the Subversion of Identity* (1989; New York: Routledge, 1990).

Benjamin Lindsay, "Boston Fraternity Raises Money for Trans Brother," *Out Magazine*, February 25, 2013, http://www.out.com/entertainment/popnography/2013/02/25/boston-fraternity-raises-money-trans-brother.

Maggie Nelson, *Argonauts* (Minneapolis: Graywolf Press, 2015).

Sarah Salih, "On Judith Butler and Performativity," in *Sexualities and Communication in Everyday Life: A Reader*, ed. Karen E. Lovaas and Mercilee M. Jenkins (Thousand Oaks, CA: Sage, 2006).

Serano, *Whipping Girl*.

Disclosure

Equaldex, "LGBT Rights in India," http://www.equaldex.com/region/india, accessed October 3, 2016.

Aaron Gardner et al., "Aging Out in the Desert: Disclosure, Acceptance, Service Use Among Midlife and Older Lesbians and Gay Men," *Journal of Homosexuality*, Special Issue on LGBT Aging, vol. 61, no 1 (2014): 129–44. *Older gay women are more fearful about outing themselves.*

Hartford Courant, "Passing for Black: Rachel Dolezal and Racial Identity," collection of articles, June 21, 2015.

J. G. Kosciw, N. Palmer, and R. Kull, "Reflecting Resiliency: Openness About Sexual Orientation and/or Gender Identity and Its Relationship to Well-Being and Educational Outcomes for LGBT Students," *American Journal of Community Psychology* 55, nos. 1–2 (March 2015): 167–78. *The huge mental health costs of not revealing the truth; but disclosure is riskier in rural areas.*

Heidi Levitt and Maria Ippolito, "Being Transgender: Navigating Minority Stressors and Developing Authentic Self-Presentation," *Psychology of Women Quarterly* 38, no. 1 (March 2014): 46–64. *Trans female-to-male see that they have more power as a man and feel guilty about that.*

Rights

Right(s)

George Coppolo, "Parental Responsibility for 16- and 17-Year-Olds," Office of Legislative Research, Connecticut General Assembly, www.cga.ct.gov, August 1, 2003.

Lawrence Furbish, "Variations from the Age of Majority in CT," Office of Legislative Research Report, Connecticut General Assembly, www.cga.ct.gov, January 28, 2003.

Gallup, "Gay and Lesbian Rights," poll taken in May 2016, http://www.gallup.com/poll/1651/gay-lesbian-rights.aspx. *For statistics on approval of homosexuality.*

Parental Rights Foundation, www.parentalrightsfoundation.org.

US Supreme Court case *Pierce v. Society of Sisters of the Holy Names of Jesus and Mary*, 1925. *Upheld the right of parents to not send their children to public school.*

Youth for Human Rights, www.youthforhumanrights.org. *For the UN Declaration of Human Rights.*

Hidden Fees

Spring 2011

Janet Mock, *Redefining Realness: My Path to Womanhood, Identity, Love & So Much More* (New York: Atria, 2014).

12/2/2011

American Psychiatric Association, *Diagnostic and Statistical Manual of Mental Disorders (DSM-5)* (Washington, DC American Psychiatric Association, 2013).

Archive for Sexology, "Harry Benjamin (1855–1986)," http://www.sexarchive.info /GESUND/ARCHIV/COLLBEN.HTM. *For background on Harry Benjamin and Magnus Hirschfeld.*

Harry Benjamin, *The Transsexual Phenomenon* (Human Outreach and Achievement Institute, 1966). Digital re-issue.

Zack Ford, "APA Revises Manual: Being Transgender Is No Longer a Mental Disorder," GLAAD, December 3, 2012.

Grant et al., *Injustice at Every Turn.*

Lambda Legal, "LGBT Advocates Issue Revised Guidelines for Hospitals Treating Transgender Patients," press release, May 25, 2016, http://www.lambdalegal .org/blog/20160525_lgbt-advocates-revise-guidelines-hospitals-trans-patients. *On hormonal effects for treatment of cis people.*

Kimberly Leonard, "Obamacare Bans LGBT Discrimination," *US News & World Report*, May 13, 2016.

Ananya Mandal, "What Is an Endocrinologist?," *News Medical*, news-medical.net, last update September 8, 2014, http://www.news-medical.net/health/What-is -an-Endocrinologist.aspx.

Serano, *Whipping Girl.*

Stryker, *Transgender History.*

US Food and Drug Administration, "Menopause and Hormones."

John A. H. Wass and Paul Stewart, "Principles of International Endocrine Practice," in *The Oxford Textbook of Endocrinology and Diabetes*, 2nd ed. (Oxford, UK: Oxford University Press, 2011).

7/25/2012

"Connecticut Law About Name Changes," Connecticut Judicial Branch Law Libraries, https://www.jud.ct.gov/LawLib/Law/namechange.htm, accessed 2016.

Thomas Page McBee, *Man Alive* (San Francisco: City Lights Books, 2014).

"Non-Discrimination Laws," Movement Advancement Project (MAP), http:// LGBTmap.org, accessed March 21, 2016.

A Story Exchange

Parent Story Exchange

C. Dhejne et al., "Mental Health and Gender Dysphoria: A Review of Literature," *International Review of Psychiatry* 28, no. 1 (February 2016): 44–57. *On the rate of depression, anxiety, and bipolar disorder in transgender people.*

Lisa Tabor Fleisher, author interview, Simsbury, CT, December 12, 2015.

Libby McKnight, facilitator for PFLAG Trans Families support group, author phone interview, Fairfax, VA, April 9, 2016, and follow-up e-mails.

Transgender Youth and Professionals Story Exchange

David Broockman and Joshua Kalla, "Durably Reducing Transphobia: A Field Experiment on Door-to-Door Canvassing," *Science* 352, no. 6282 (April 8, 2016): 220–24.

Sunnivie Brydum, "North Carolina Governor Signs Repeal of LGBT Protections," *Advocate*, March 23, 2016, http://www.advocate.com/politics/2016/3/23/north-carolina-house-strikes-down-lgbt-protections-statewide.

Cordelia Fine, *Delusions of Gender: How Our Minds, Society, and Neurosexism Create Difference* (New York: W. W. Norton, 2011), 36.

Martha M. Lauzen, "It's a Man's (Celluloid) World: Portrayals of Female Characters in the Top 100 Films of 2015," *2014 On-Screen Representations*, Center for the Study of Women in Television and Film, San Diego State University, 2016.

———, "The Celluloid Ceiling: Behind-the-Scenes Employment of Women on the Top 100, 250, and 500 Films of 2015," *2015 Celluloid Ceiling*, Center for the Study of Women in Television and Film, San Diego State University, 2016.

Dru Levasseur, attorney and director of the Transgender Rights Project, Lambda Legal, author phone interview, April 16, 2016, and follow-up e-mails.

Mal M., journalist, author phone interview, May 10, 2016.

Oscar Olivera Soens, trans advocate and college student, author phone interview, May 3, 2016.

Alyssandra Taylor, trans artist, activist, and actress, author phone interview, May 17, 2016.

A Note from the Series Editor

Conversation is at the heart of politics. It is at the heart of change. And it is at the heart of families.

Over the past decade we have heard politicians repeatedly say, "These are conversations people need to have around the kitchen table." The phrase is usually used about topics—race, in particular—that require a change of hearts and minds, and require more than legislation or judicial decisions to solve; topics that are difficult and approached best by dialogue, openness, and honesty. As clichéd as this phrase has become—and to be fair, it is also used as a way to avoid discussing some of these issues publicly—there is truth to the claim that change happens through conversation. *At the Broken Places: A Mother and Trans Son Pick Up the Pieces* is a beautiful example of a conversation—between book covers, though, not around a kitchen table—that can transform hearts, feelings, and even how we live in the world.

In this coauthored book, Mary Collins and her son, Donald Collins, share their feelings, pain, hopes, and frustration with each other, discussing their often conflicting feelings about Donald transitioning, in his teens, to being a transgender man. The emotional vividness and candor of these pieces—which speak to one another, across one another, and sometimes at one another—are riveting, occasionally upsetting, and ultimately illuminating. This is the emotional clarity—even as Mary and Donald sort through their myriad feelings about each other—that is the essence of social change. *At the Broken Places* is not a superficial, feel-good journey but rather a book that pushes us, through the emotional evolution of its writers, to face emotions and concerns we might be tempted to side-step or avoid. In the past two decades there have been a plethora of books dealing with transgender lives, histories, theory, medical and psychological issues, many of which have been excellent. There have been books addressing parents, concerns about transgender children, and how to "come out" as transgender to family and communities. *At the Broken Places* breaks from the usual genre limitations of these past works to take us into the hearts and minds of a mother and son who are learning to love one another all over again.

—MICHAEL BRONSKI
Series Editor, Queer Action/Queer Ideas